# The Eastern Christian Churches

*Finito di stampare nel mese di luglio 1993 dalla Tipolitografia 2000 s.a.s.*
*di De Magistris e Ceccacci & C. - 00047 Marino (Roma)*
*Via Marcantonio Colonna, s.n.c. - tel.-fax 06/938.46.59*

# The Eastern Christian Churches
## A Brief Survey (1993 Edition)

✝ ✝ ✝ ✝ ✝

### Ronald G. Roberson, CSP

Edizioni «Orientalia Christiana»

1993

Cover design: Thomas Kane, CSP

ISBN 88-7210-293-6

ms: Eastern Orthodox Churches

EDIZIONI «ORIENTALIA CHRISTIANA»
Pontificio Istituto Orientale
Piazza S. Maria Maggiore, 7
00185 Roma, Italy

# TABLE OF CONTENTS

# Foreword

Eight years have elapsed since Fr. Ronald Roberson gave his first conference on the Eastern Churches at the Paulist novitiate in Oak Ridge, New Jersey. The former managing editor of Edizioni «Orientalia Christiana» Fr. James Lee Dugan, SJ, encouraged him to prepare it for publication. In this way, there appeared in 1986 the first edition of *The Eastern Christian Churches*, hardly more than a brochure of 40 pages all told. It was a very lucky piece of advice Fr. Dugan gave. Since then the work has enjoyed great success, witnessed by the fact that it became a best-seller of Edizioni «Orientalia Christiana».

The present is the fourth, revised and updated edition, with two informative appendixes and an index of churches and their heads.

It is our hope that through this and other publications of the Edizioni «Orientalia Christiana», (the biannual review *Orientalia Christiana Periodica*, and monographic works published in two series: *Orientalia Christiana Analecta* and *Kanonika*), the Christian East will be better known and cherished.

Jaroslaw Dziewicki
Managing Editor

# Introduction

Many western Christians are baffled by the complexity of the Christian east, which can appear to be a bewildering array of national churches and ethnic jurisdictions. The purpose of this survey is to provide a clear overview of the Eastern Churches for the non-specialist by furnishing basic information about each of them and indicating the relationships among them. Each church is placed in its historical, geographical, doctrinal, and liturgical context. Because this book is primarily intended for an English-speaking audience, details are also provided regarding the presence each of these churches in North America, Britain, and Australia.

The principle used here for the classification of these churches is communion. That is, it describes groups of churches that are in full communion with one another, rather than treating them according to other criteria such as liturgical tradition.

This approach yields four distinct and separate Eastern Christian communions: 1) the Assyrian Church of the East, which is not in communion with any other church; 2) the five Oriental Orthodox Churches, which, although each is fully independent, are in communion with one another; 3) the Orthodox Church, which is a communion of national or regional churches all of which recognize the Patriarch of Constantinople as a point of unity enjoying certain rights and privileges; and 4) the Eastern Catholic Churches, all of which are in communion with the Church of Rome and its bishop. The order in which these four communions are listed should not be vested with any particular significance. It reflects only the chronological sequence in which they emerged as distinct entities.

The only exception to this rule is the Orthodox Churches of Irregular Status (section III,D). They have been included as a sub-category of the Orthodox Church, but they are not in full communion with it. All of them are of Orthodox origin, but today the Orthodox view them as at least uncanonical if not fully schismatic.

I have endeavored in this book to present these churches as they are, and to describe disputed matters without making judgments as to the rightness or wrongness of the various points of view. For instance, the order in which the autocephalous Orthodox churches should be listed presents a problem because the Orthodox are not in unanimous agreement among themselves as to the precedence of their churches after the four ancient patriarchates. I have listed them in an order which corresponds to that of the Patriarchate of Constantinople and most other Orthodox Churches, and have added the two churches which have been granted autocephalous status by the Moscow Patriarchate, but are not recognized as such by Constantinople. The four ancient patriarchates are followed by the five patriarchates of more recent origin, and then by the other autocephalous churches which do not have the rank of patriarchate.

Another sensitive matter is the status of the Orthodox Church in America, which I have included among the autocephalous Orthodox churches. In doing this I am aware that the OCA is not recognized as an autocephalous church by Constantinople and most other Orthodox churches. This is why it is not allowed to take part in such pan-Orthodox activities as international dialogues with other Christian churches. Nevertheless, it functions as an autocephalous church, and its inclusion in the American Standing Conference of Canonical Orthodox Bishops indicates that it has achieved a certain level of legitimacy among other Orthodox churches in the United States. The problem of the unity of Orthodox faithful in the diaspora is a serious one which is to be taken up at the future Pan-Orthodox Council. My inclusion of the Orthodox Church in America among the autocephalous churches does not mean that I am advocating its autocephalous status against those who are opposed to it. As on other controverted questions, it is not my intention to take a position on the problem, but only to describe it.

The membership statistics provided for these churches must be treated with caution. Many Eastern Churches exist in areas where no census has been taken, or where the size of church membership would have explosive political implications. Thus one is forced to rely on estimates which at times are of limited value.

In the case of churches which are members of the World Council of Churches, I usually report the figures which were provided by them to the WCC and published in its 1985 revised *Handbook of Member Churches*, edited by Ans J. van der Bent. For other churches and jurisdictions I have most often relied on the data provided in *The World Christian Encyclopedia*, edited by D. Barrett, and published in 1982. This work claims to present the most accurate statistics on church membership available. For the Eastern Catholic Churches, I have taken figures exclusively from the 1993 *Annuario Pontificio*, the annual yearbook of the Vatican. It provides official membership statistics for every Catholic diocese. I have added up the membership figures provided for each diocese of the various Eastern Catholic Churches and rounded off the sum to the next highest thousand. It should be kept in mind that these figures will be lower than the real membership of churches which have a significant presence in the diaspora. This is because they do not include faithful of those churches which, lacking sufficient numbers to form their own dioceses, come under the jurisdiction of the local Latin bishops.

Although I have provided membership statistics for each of the churches listed, in most cases I have only furnished the number of parishes in the English-speaking world. This is due not only to the fact that such statistics are hard to obtain, but also because it is often difficult to distinguish ethnic identity from church membership. In the case of the Eastern Catholic Churches, however, I report the number of faithful indicated in the 1993 *Annuario Pontificio*.

It may be noticed that the entries for some smaller churches are more extensive than those of some larger or more prestigious ones. This is because I have endeavored to supply more extensive information regarding some churches whose histories, etc., are less known and less readily accessible. A number of the most important works in English which treat the larger churches are indicated in the bibliography.

I have only treated the ecumenical relationships between these four communions in a passing way in the main text, although I have provided basic information about the christological controversy between the Oriental Orthodox Churches and those churches which

accepted the Council of Chalcedon. The Roman Catholic and Orthodox Churches have been engaged in an international theological
dialogue since 1980. A series of unofficial consultations between the
Roman Catholic and Oriental Orthodox Churches has been under-
way since the 1970's, and significant common statements have been
issued by Popes and Oriental Orthodox hierarchs concerning
christological doctrine and other issues dividing their churches. A
commission for dialogue between the Catholic and Coptic churches
has been meeting since 1973, and a new dialogue with the Malankara
Orthodox Syrian Church in India was inaugurated in October 1989.
Moreover, the Orthodox Church has been engaged in dialogue with
the Anglican Communion since 1976, and an official dialogue began
between the Orthodox Church and the Oriental Orthodox Churches
in December 1985. Sources on these dialogues can be found in the
bibliography, along with books on other aspects of the Eastern
Churches.

This fourth edition includes as appendices two articles on ecumenical themes that I have published elsewhere. The first, entitled
"Catholic-Orthodox Relations in Post-Communist Europe: Ghosts
from the Past and Challenges for the Future," is a conference given at
Rome's Centro Pro Unione on March 18, 1993. It was published in
the *Centro Pro Unione Semi-Annual Bulletin* Number 43 (Spring 1993)
17-31. The original text has been very slightly revised for this edition.
The second article, "The Contemporary Relationship between the
Roman Catholic and Oriental Orthodox Churches," first appeared as
"The Modern Roman Catholic-Oriental Orthodox Dialogue" in *One
in Christ* 21 (1985) 238-254. In an updated form and with the present
title it appeared in *The Vienna Dialogue: Five Pro Oriente Consultations
with Oriental Orthodoxy*, Booklet Nr. 1, Vienna: Pro Oriente [1991], pp.
23-38. Here it has again been updated and slightly revised. Much of
the material presented in this edition on the Eastern Catholic
Churches will also appear in the forthcoming *Encyclopedia of Catholicism*, to be published by HarperCollins under the general editorship
of Richard P. McBrien.

Any constructive comments that readers may wish to make on
this text are welcomed, as well as updated information which could

be considered for inclusion in subsequent editions of this book. Letters can be addressed to the author at St. Paul's College, 3015 Fourth Street NE, Washington, DC 20017 USA.

Momentous changes have taken place in the lives of many of these churches in the three years since the third edition of this work was published. I have tried to provide updated accounts of their current situation which in many cases remains very fluid, changing from day to day.

I would like to extend my sincere thanks to the many people I consulted while preparing this survey and its three previous editions. They have helped me to cover an extremely varied and complex history, and to present it as clearly as possible. I have done my best to remain objective and fair in treating what at times are tragic and painful situations in the history of these churches and the relationships between them. I hope that this survey will in some small way help western Christians to understand more about our sisters and brothers in the east, so that one day the Church might learn, as in the image often evoked by Pope John Paul II, to again breathe fully with two lungs, one eastern and one western.

June 27, 1993

# I. The Assyrian Church of the East

It is not known exactly when Christianity first took root in upper Mesopotamia, but a Christian presence had certainly been established there by the mid-2nd century. In the 3rd century, the area was conquered by the Persians. Although this was to be a multi-ethnic church, the Assyrian people traditionally played a central role in its ecclesial life. Its geographical location caused it to become known simply as "The Church of the East."

Around the year 300, the bishops were first organized into an ecclesiastical structure under the leadership of a Catholicos, the bishop of the Persian royal capital at Seleucia-Ctesiphon. He later received the additional title of Patriarch.

In the 5th century, the Church of the East gravitated towards the radical Antiochene form of christology that had been articulated by Theodore of Mopsuestia and Nestorius, and fell out of communion with the church in the Roman Empire. This was due in part to the significant influx of Nestorian Christians into Persia that took place following the condemnation of Nestorian christology by the Council of Ephesus in 431, and the expulsion of Nestorians from the Roman Empire by Emperor Zeno (474-491). In addition, the Persian Christians needed to distance themselves from the official church of the Roman Empire, with which Persia was frequently at war. In this way they were able to maintain their Christian faith while avoiding suspicions that they were collaborating with the Roman enemy.

Synods in the 5th century also decreed that celibacy should be obligatory for no one in this church, including bishops. A number of bishops and even patriarchs were married until the early 6th century, when the decision was taken to ordain only celibate monks to the episcopate. Priests, however, have always been allowed to marry, even after ordination.

The Church of the East was always a minority in largely Zoroastrian Persia, but nevertheless it flourished for many centuries, with its rich scholarly activity centered on the famous school of Nisibis.

The church expanded through missionary activity into areas as far away as India, Tibet, China, and Mongolia. This continued even after the Mesopotamian homeland was conquered by the Muslim Arabs in the 7th century. The Patriarchate was moved to the new city of Baghdad after it became the capital in 766. By 1318 there were some 30 metropolitan sees and 200 suffragan dioceses. But during the invasions of Tamerlane in the late 14th century, these Christians were almost annihilated. By the 16th century, they had been reduced to a small community of Assyrians in what is now eastern Turkey. The church was then further weakened by the formation of a Catholic counterpart known as the Chaldean Catholic Church [see IV.B.1].

During World War I, the Assyrians suffered massive deportations and massacres at the hands of the Turks who suspected them of supporting the British enemy. About one third of the Assyrian population perished. Most of the survivors fled south into Iraq hoping to be protected by the British. But in 1933, after the end of the British mandate in Iraq, a clash between Assyrians and Iraqi troops ended in another massacre and further scattering of the community. The Iraqi authorities then stripped Assyrian Patriarch Mar Simon XXIII of his citizenship and expelled him. He went into exile in San Francisco, California, USA.

In 1964 a dispute arose within the church, triggered by Mar Simon's decision to adopt the Gregorian calendar. But the real issue was the person of Mar Simon and the centuries-old practice by which he was elected. Since 1450, the office of patriarch had been hereditary within one family, usually being passed down from uncle to nephew. This often produced unqualified leaders of the church who at times were elected at a very young age: Mar Simon himself had been elected at age 12. The dissidents also held that a patriarch was needed who could live with his community in Iraq.

Those opposed to Mar Simon were supported by Mar Thomas Darmo, the Assyrian Metropolitan of India. In 1968 he traveled from India to Baghdad and ordained three new bishops. They then met in synod and elected him patriarch over against Mar Simon. Mar

Thomas Darmo died in the following year, and was succeeded in 1970 by Mar Addai of Baghdad.

But in 1973 Mar Simon resigned as patriarch and married. As no successor could be agreed upon, the Assyrian bishops in communion with him attempted to persuade him to resume his office despite his marriage. But in the midst of these negotiations, on November 6, 1975, Mar Simon was assassinated in San Jose, California. The bishop of Teheran, Iran, was elected patriarch in 1976 and adopted the name Mar Denkha IV. He took up residence in Morton Grove, Illinois, USA.

Mar Denkha made it clear that with his election, the patriarchal dynasty had ended. This removed the major reason for the schism between the two groups, each of which now has about the same number of bishops. Although the rift has not yet been healed, recent meetings between bishops of the two sides appear to have made substantial progress towards resolving the dispute.

The Assyrians accept only the first two ecumenical councils and officially adhere to Nestorian doctrine, according to which in Christ there are two natures and two "qnoma" (a Syriac term with no Greek equivalent which refers to an individual concrete nature), in one person. Even so, the synod of bishops has requested that they not be referred to as the "Nestorian Church," since this term has been used in the past to insult them. The Assyrians are not in communion with any other church.

The East Syrian rite of the Assyrian Church appears to have been an independent development from the ancient Syriac liturgy of Edessa. It may also preserve elements of an ancient Persian rite which has been lost. Services are still held predominantly in Syriac.

In North America, Mar Aprim Khamis presides over the Diocese of Eastern United States (8908 Birch Avenue, Morton Grove, Illinois 60053), and Mar Bawai Soro is Bishop of the Western United States (680 Minnesota Avenue, San Jose, California 95125). Altogether there are 15 parishes and one mission in the country. Mar Emmanuel Joseph is Bishop of Canada where there are three parishes (165 Thistle Down Boulevard, Etobicoke, Ontario M9V 1J7). Assyrians in Australia, who have four parishes, are headed by Mar Meelis Zaia

(6718 North Campbell, P.O. Box 621, Fairfield NSW 2165). There is also one Assyrian parish in London.

LOCATION: Iraq, Iran, Syria, Lebanon, North America, Australia, India.

HEAD: Mar Denkha IV (born 1935, elected 1976)
Title: Catholicos-Patriarch of the Church of the East
Residence: Morton Grove, Illinois, USA
MEMBERSHIP: 400,000


## The Thomas Christians

When the Portuguese arrived in India at the end of the 15th century, they encountered a Christian community claiming to have been founded by the Apostle Thomas when he evangelized India following the death and resurrection of Christ. Located on the southwest coast, in what is now Kerala State, they were fully integrated into Indian society as a separate caste. They were in full communion with the Assyrian Church of the East, which in early centuries had regularly sent bishops to India to ordain deacons and priests. In the 8th century India received its own Metropolitan who was assigned the tenth place in the Assyrian hierarchy. But because the Metropolitans generally did not speak the local language, real jurisdiction was placed in the hands of an Indian priest with the title "Archdeacon of All India." He was effectively the civil and religious superior of the entire community until the arrival of the Portuguese.

Portuguese colonization was the beginning of a sad history of forced latinization which caused unrest and schisms among the Thomas Christians. Today their descendants, who number about 5,000,000, are divided into five oriental churches, including about 15,000 who still belong to the Assyrian Church of the East. For the others see The Syrian Orthodox Church [II.D], The Malankara Orthodox Syrian Church [II.E], The Syro-Malabar Catholic Church [IV.B.2], and The Syro-Malankara Catholic Church [IV.C.5].

Another interesting feature of the Thomas Christians is the existence among them of a distinct ethnic community known as the

"Southists," or "Knanaya." According to tradition, their origins can be traced to a group of 72 Jewish Christian families who immigrated to India from Mesopotamia in the year 345 AD. There is historical evidence to support this claim. The descendants of these ancient immigrants, who do not intermarry with those outside the community and now number about 200,000, are divided into two ethnic dioceses in Kerala, one belonging to the Syro-Malabar Catholic Church and the other to the Syrian Orthodox Patriarchate.

## II. THE ORIENTAL ORTHODOX CHURCHES

The term "Oriental Orthodox Churches" is now generally used to describe a group of five ancient eastern churches. Although they are in communion with one another, each is fully independent and possesses many distinctive traditions.

The common element among these churches is their rejection of the christological definition of the Council of Chalcedon (451), which asserted that Christ is one person in two natures, undivided and unconfused. For them, to say that Christ has two natures was to overemphasize the duality in Christ, and to compromise the unity of his person. Yet they reject the classical monophysite position of Eutyches, who held that Christ's humanity was absorbed into his single divine nature. They prefer the formula of St. Cyril of Alexandria, who spoke of "the one incarnate nature of the Word of God" (μία φύσις τοῦ Θεοῦ Λόγου σεσαρκωμένη).

During the period following Chalcedon, those who rejected the council's teaching made up a significant portion of the Christians in the Byzantine Empire. Today, however, they are greatly reduced in number. Some of these churches have existed for centuries in areas where there is a non-Christian majority, and more recently others have been suffering from many decades of persecution by communist governments.

Because they denied Chalcedon's definition of two natures in Christ, these Christians have often erroneously been called "monophysites," from the Greek word meaning "one nature." The group has also been referred to as "The Lesser Eastern Churches," "The Ancient Oriental Churches," "The Non-Chalcedonian Churches," or "The Pre-Chalcedonian Churches." Today it is widely recognized by theologians and church leaders on both sides that the christological differences between the Oriental Orthodox and those who accepted Chalcedon were only verbal, and that in fact both parties profess the same faith in Christ using different formulas.

## II. A. The Armenian Apostolic Church

Ancient Armenia was located in present-day eastern Turkey and in bordering areas of the former Soviet Union and Iran. This country became the first nation to adopt Christianity as its state religion when King Tiridates III was converted to the Christian faith by St. Gregory the Illuminator at the beginning of the 4th century. A cathedral was soon built at Etchmiadzin which to this day remains the center of the Armenian Church. It is widely believed that the monk St. Mesrob invented the Armenian alphabet around the year 406, making it possible for the Bible to be translated into that language.

In 506 an Armenian synod rejected the christological teachings of the Council of Chalcedon, which no Armenian bishop had attended. At that time the Armenian Church was more concerned with countering the nestorianizing tendencies of the neighboring church in the Persian Empire.

Long a vulnerable buffer state between the hostile Roman and Persian empires, the ancient Armenian kingdom was destroyed in the 11th century. Many Armenians then fled to Cilicia (south central Asia Minor), where a new Armenian kingdom was established. Here the Armenians had extensive contacts with the Latin Crusaders. Although this new kingdom also ceased to exist by the 14th century and the Armenian people were dispersed, they survived in spite of foreign domination. Their identity as a people centered on their language and their church.

In the late 19th and early 20th centuries, the Armenians in Turkey suffered a series of massacres and expulsions which led to the death of large numbers of them. It is widely believed that altogether between 1.5 and 2 million Armenians died in this tragedy. The survivors fled to neighboring countries and to Istanbul.

Today the Armenian Apostolic Church is centered in the Republic of Armenia which declared its independence on 23 September 1991. The holy city of Etchmiadzin, the ancient residence of the Armenian Catholicos, is near Yerevan, the capital. The collapse of Soviet communism has provided conditions for a renaissance of this ancient church in its homeland. New dioceses and parishes are being opened, new organizations founded, religious periodicals published, and religious instruction has been introduced in the schools. But the church is experiencing a lack of sufficient clergy, and feels threatened by the new activity of other religious groups which are now free to function in the country. The war with Azerbaijan over the Armenian-inhabited region of Nagorno-Karabagh has created catastrophic economic conditions and much suffering for the Armenian people. In February 1993 Catholicos Vasken and the head of the Islamic community in Azerbaijan jointly declared that religious differences were not the cause of the conflict.

The Armenian liturgy reflects the Syriac, Jerusalem, and Byzantine traditions. While a distinctive Armenian liturgical tradition was being formed in the 5th to the 7th centuries, there was strong liturgical influence from Syria and Jerusalem. Later there was a period of byzantinization, and finally, during the Middle Ages, many Latin usages were adopted.

Although the Armenian Catholicos in Etchmiadzin is recognized by all Armenian Orthodox as the spiritual head of their church, three other Armenian jurisdictions have emerged over the centuries. The two Catholicosates are administratively independent, while the two Patriarchates are dependent on Etchmiadzin. *The Catholicosate of Etchmiadzin* has jurisdiction over Armenians throughout the former USSR and much of the diaspora, including Iraq, India, Egypt, Sudan, Ethiopia, Europe, Australia and the Americas. I. includes about 5,000,000 faithful. *The Patriarchate of Jerusalem* has its headquarters at St. James monastery in that city, and is responsible for the holy places which belong to the Armenian Church. It includes the 10,000 Armenian faithful in Israel and Jordan, and is under the pastoral guidance of Patriarch Torkom Manoogian (born 1919, elected 1990). *The Patriarchate of Constantinople* has jurisdiction over those Armenians who remain in Turkey. In 1914 this patriarchate included 12 archdioceses, 27 dioceses, and six monasteries with approximately 1,350,000 faithful. Today only the Patriarchate itself remains, with a flock of about 40,000 in Istanbul. Patriarch Karekin II Kazandjian (born 1927) was elected in 1990. *The Catholicosate of Cilicia*, now based in Antelias, Lebanon, has jurisdiction in Lebanon, Syria, Cyprus, Iran, and Greece, and has about 800,000 members. The present Catholicos is Karekin Sarkissian (born 1932, elected 1983). Cilicia has had a history of tension with Etchmiadzin, and both maintain separate jurisdictions in North America.

The Armenian Apostolic Church currently maintains four seminaries: Kevorkian Seminary in Etchmiadzin, a seminary of the Catholicosate of Cilicia in Bikfaya, Lebanon, St. James Seminary in Jerusalem, and St. Nersess Seminary in New Rochelle, New York, which is associated with St. Vladimir's Orthodox Seminary in nearby Crestwood, NY.

The Catholicosate of Etchmiadzin has bishops throughout the diaspora. The Armenians in the United Kingdom, who have three parishes, are under the pastoral supervision of Bishop Yegishe Gizirian (St. Sarkis Church, Iverna Gardens, London W8 6TP). Bishop Aghan Baliozian is Primate of Australia and New Zealand (Holy Resurrection Armenian Church, 10 Marquarie Street, PO Box 694, Chatswood NSW 2067). There are parishes in Sydney and Melbourne. In North America, the Eastern USA Diocese (St. Vartan's Cathedral, 630 Second Avenue, New York, N.Y. 10016) is headed by Archbishop Khajag Barsamian, while Archbishop Vatche Hovsepian of Los Angeles is Primate of the Western USA Diocese (1201 North Vine Street, Hollywood, CA 90038). Altogether there are 65 parishes in the USA. The Diocese of Canada (615 Stuart Avenue, Montréal, Québec H2V 3H2), which has five parishes, is under the pastoral care of Bishop Hovnan Derderian.

The Catholicosate of Cilicia also has two dioceses in the United States: the Prelacy of the Eastern United States and Canada is headed by Archbishop Mesrob Ashdjian (138 East 39th Street, New York, NY 10016), and the Western Prelacy is presided over by Archbishop Datev Sarkissian (4401 Russell Avenue, Los Angeles, CA 90027). Altogether there are 33 parishes the USA, and 4 in Canada.

LOCATION:Armenia, large diaspora

HEAD: Catholicos Vasken I (born 1908, elected 1955)

Title: Catholicos-Supreme Patriarch of All Armenians
Residence: Etchmiadzin, Armenia
Membership: 6,000,000

## II. B. The Coptic Orthodox Church

The foundation of the church in Egypt is closely associated with St. Mark the Evangelist who, according to tradition, was martyred in Alexandria in 63 A.D. Eventually Egypt became a Christian nation and Alexandria an extremely important center of theological reflection. Moreover, monks in the Egyptian desert provided the first models for the Christian monastic tradition, having been nourished by the spiritual insights of the early "desert fathers."

But the christological teachings of the Council of Chalcedon in 451, partially because of opposition to Byzantine domination, were rejected by much of the Egyptian hierarchy and faithful. Persecutions intended to force acceptance only reinforced the resistance. Eventually a separate "Coptic" (from the Arabic and Greek word for "Egyptian") Church emerged with a distinct theological and liturgical tradition. From the 5th to the 9th centuries the Greek Patriarchs lived in the city of Alexandria, while the Coptic Patriarchs resided in the desert monastery of St. Macarius.

After the Arab invasion in 641, the Copts slowly diminished in numbers, becoming a minority in Egypt around the year 850. Arabic replaced Coptic as the official language of the country in the 8th century. Islamic rule was marked by long periods of persecution, but also by periods of relative freedom, during which the church flourished again and produced outstanding theological and spiritual works in Arabic.

The Copts are the largest Christian community in the Middle East, and are still a significant minority in Egypt. There is some evidence that the official membership figure reported below is underestimated, and that there may be as many as six million Copts in the country.

There are many separate Coptic schools in Egypt, and a Sunday School movement flourishes. Presently an encouraging revival of monasticism is taking place, and many young monks, involved in agriculture and publishing, inhabit the ancient desert monasteries. There are currently twelve monasteries with close to 600 monks, and six convents with about 300 nuns. The largest concentration of monasteries is at Wadi Natrun, about sixty miles northwest of Cairo.

The Coptic Church's main seminary is in Cairo next to St. Mark's Cathedral. About half of the church's priests were educated there, and many laypeople participate in evening courses in scripture and theology. A Coptic Institute of Higher Studies, founded in 1954 and situated at the patriarchal compound, is an important ecumenical center for the study of the Coptic Christian tradition.

The recent rise of Islamic fundamentalism in Egypt has created new problems for the Coptic Church. Following anti-Coptic outbursts by fundamentalists in the late 1970's, President Sadat in 1981 placed Pope Shenouda III under house arrest in one of the desert monasteries. He was not released until 1985. It was generally surmised that this action resulted from the government's need to appear even-handed in dealing with conflicting groups. Nevertheless, this interference in the affairs of the Coptic Church disturbed many Egyptian Christians, and the activity of Islamic fundamentalists appears to be increasing.

The Coptic liturgy grew from the original Greek rite of Alexandria, developing by the 4th century its own native characteristics. This process took place mainly in the monasteries, and to this day the Coptic liturgy has many monastic characteristics. It is celebrated in both Coptic and Arabic.

A Coptic diocese of North America has been established, presided over directly by Pope Shenouda III. There are 50 communities in the USA and 12 in Canada. Further information can be obtained from Rev. Dr. Gabriel A. Abdelsayed, 429 West Side Avenue, Jersey City, NJ 07304. In Australia there are 14 Coptic parishes, also under the direct supervision of Pope Shenouda. The Secretary of the Coptic Board of Deacons can be reached at 70 Wollongong Road, Arncliffe, NSW 2205. There are also six Coptic communities in Britain, and one

in Ireland. The Secretary of the Coptic Church Council is Dr. Fuad
Megally, 509 Duncan House, Dolphin Square, London SW1.

LOCATION: Egypt and diaspora in Europe, Africa, Australia, the
Americas
HEAD: Pope Shenouda III (born 1923, elected 1971)
Title: Pope of Alexandria, Patriarch of the See of St. Mark
Residence: Cairo, Egypt
MEMBERSHIP: 3,900,000

## II. C. The Ethiopian Orthodox Church

According to an ancient tradition, the first great evangelizer of the
Ethiopians was St. Frumentius, who had been ordained a bishop by
St. Athanasius of Alexandria. He and other Coptic missionaries
made many converts to the faith in the mid-4th century, including
the king. Christianity soon became the official religion of the country, although paganism was still widespread.

Towards the end of the 5th century, the "Nine Saints" arrived in
Ethiopia and began missionary activities. They were most probably
of Syrian origin, and had left their country because of their opposition to Chalcedonian christology. This, along with its traditional
links with the Copts in Egypt, probably explains the origin of the
Ethiopian Church's rejection of Chalcedon. The Nine Saints are
credited with introducing the monastic tradition into Ethiopia, and
with having made a substantial contribution to the development of
Ge'ez religious literature by translating the Bible and religious works
into that classical Ethiopian language. Monasteries quickly sprang
up throughout the country and became important intellectual
centers.

The Ethiopian Church reached its zenith in the 15th century when
much creative theological and spiritual literature was produced, and
the church was engaged in extensive missionary activity.

The very negative experience of contact with Portuguese Roman
Catholic missionaries in the 16th century [see Ethiopian Catholic

Church, IV.C.3] was followed by centuries of isolation from which the Ethiopian Church has only recently emerged.

This church is unique in retaining several Jewish practices such as circumcision and the observance of dietary laws and Saturday sabbath as well as Sunday. This is probably due to the fact that the earliest presence of Christianity in Ethiopia had come directly from Palestine through southern Arabia. There have also been some unusual christological developments (not officially accepted), including a school of thought which holds that the union of Christ's divine and human natures took place only upon his anointing at Baptism.

Ge'ez, the ancient Ethiopian language, has traditionally been used in the liturgy, which is of Alexandrian (Coptic) origin and influenced by the Syriac tradition. However, a translation of the liturgy into modern Amharic is being used increasingly in the parishes. A strong monastic tradition continues.

From ancient times, all bishops in Ethiopia were Egyptian Copts appointed by the Coptic Patriarchate. Indeed, for many centuries the only bishop in Ethiopia was the Coptic Metropolitan. By popular demand, in 1929 four native Ethiopian bishops were elected to assist the ethnic Egyptian Metropolitan. In 1951 for the first time an ethnic Ethiopian Metropolitan was chosen by the Ethiopian clergy and laity. In 1959 the Coptic Patriarchate confirmed the independence of the Ethiopian Church, raising the rank of its head to Patriarch.

There was a theological college at the University of Addis Ababa until it was closed in 1974. In the same year, the church established Saint Paul Theological College in Addis Ababa which provides a four-year program of higher theological education. It has long been common for many Ethiopian Orthodox men to ask for ordination; it was estimated in 1988 that there were 250,000 clergymen in the country. In order to provide them with an adequate level of education, six "Clergy Training Centers" have recently been established in various parts of Ethiopia. Every parish is now expected to have a Sunday School program.

Especially in recent years, the Ethiopian Church has assumed an active role in serving those in need. It has sponsored relief efforts on behalf of refugees and victims of drought, and a number of church-sponsored orphanages have been set up.

The Ethiopian Orthodox Church was the state religion of the country until the Marxist revolution of 1974 which overthrew the Emperor and placed Colonel Mengistu Haile Mariam at the head of government. Soon after the revolution, church and state were officially separated and most church land was nationalized. This signalled the beginning of a campaign against all the religious groups in the country.

Following the collapse of the communist government in May 1991, Patriarch Merkorios (elected in 1988) was accused of collaboration with the Mengistu regime. In September, under pressure, he resigned his duties as Patriarch. On 5 July 1992, the Holy Synod elected Abune Paulos as fifth Patriarch of the Ethiopian Orthodox Church. He had been imprisoned for seven years by the Marxist authorities after Patriarch Theophilos (deposed in 1976 and murdered in prison in 1979) ordained him a bishop without government approval in 1975. Paulos was released in 1983 and had spent the intervening years in the United States. Meanwhile, Patriarch Merkorios, who took refuge in Kenya, challenged the election of Paulos, and demanded that he be reinstated in office. By spring 1993 this dispute had not yet been resolved.

The Ethiopian province of Eritrea achieved independence in 1993. An Ethiopian Orthodox bishop continues to reside in Asmara with the title Archbishop of Eritrea. But the idea of establishing a fully independent Eritrean Orthodox Church was gaining ground at the time of Eritrean independence.

The total membership figure reported below was provided by the WCC. But some credible sources in Ethiopia believe that the true figure may be as high as 30 million, based on estimates that the Ethiopian Orthodox make up about 60% of the total population of 55 million.

In Australia the Ethiopian community can be reached through Fr. Tashoma Ezeryhuen Malaka Tabor at 42 Wilkins Street, Yarraville VIC 3013. An Ethiopian Orthodox Diocese of the Western Hemisphere (established in 1951) includes a significant number of converts in the West Indies. It is presided over by Archbishop Yesehaq (140-142 West 176th Street, Bronx, New York 10451), who also oversees three parishes in Britain. There are about 90,000 members in the Western Hemisphere. Archbishop Yesehaq has joined Patriarch Merkorios in resisting the election of Patriarch Paulos, and in September 1992 formally broke all ties between his Archdiocese and the Patriarchate in Addis Ababa.

LOCATION:Ethiopia, small diaspora
HEAD: Patriarch Paulos (born 1935, elected 1992)
Title: Patriarch of the Ethiopian Orthodox Church
Residence: Addis Ababa, Ethiopia
MEMBERSHIP: 16,000,000

## II. D. The Syrian Orthodox Church

The Syrian Church traces its origins back to the early Christian community at Antioch, which is mentioned in the book of Acts. The Antiochene Church became one of the great centers of Christianity in the early centuries. But the Council of Chalcedon in 451 provoked a split in the community. The council's teachings were enforced by the Byzantine imperial authorities in the cities, but they were largely rejected in the countryside.

In the 6th century, the Bishop of Edessa, Jacob Baradai, ordained many bishops and priests to carry on the faith of those who rejected Chalcedon in the face of imperial opposition. Consequently, this church became known as "Jacobite," with its own liturgy (called "West Syrian" or "Antiochene") and other traditions using the Syriac language spoken by the common people. Some communities were also established outside the Byzantine Empire in Persia.

The conquest of the area by the Persians and later the Arabs ended Byzantine persecution, and created conditions favoring further development of the Syrian Church. There was a great revival of Syrian Orthodox scholarship in the Middle Ages, when the community possessed flourishing schools of theology, philosophy, history, and science. At its height, the church included twenty metropolitan sees and 103 dioceses extending as far to the east as Afghanistan. There is also evidence of communities of Syrian Orthodox faithful without bishops as distant as Turkestan and Sinkiang during this period.

But the Mongol invasions under Tamerlane in the late 14th century, during which most Syrian churches and monasteries were destroyed, marked the beginning of a long decline. Terrible losses were suffered again during and after World War I because of persecutions and massacres in eastern Turkey. This led to a widespread dispersion of the community.

Even now the Syrian Orthodox population is shifting. In the 1950's and 1960's many emigrated from Iraq and Syria to Lebanon. Within Iraq, they have been moving from the northern city of Mosul to Baghdad. The most serious erosion of the community has taken place in southeast Turkey, where only a few Syrian Orthodox remain. Earlier in this century many Syrian Orthodox also immigrated to Western Europe and the Americas for economic and political reasons.

The Syrians have a strong monastic tradition, and a few monasteries survive in southeastern Turkey and other parts of the Middle East. A monastery has recently been founded in the Netherlands, the only one of its kind in the diaspora.

The Syrian Patriarchs resided in Antioch until 1034. Since that time they have resided in Mar Barsauma monastery (1034-1293), Der ez-Za'faran monastery (1293-1924), Homs, Syria (1924-1959), and finally Damascus (since 1959).

Some theological education is still provided by the monasteries. But St. Ephrem Syrian Orthodox Seminary is the major theological institute of the Patriarchate. It was founded in Mosul, Iraq, in 1939, but was moved to Lebanon in the 1960's. New facilities were built at Atchaneh, near Beirut, in 1968, but the outbreak of civil war in Lebanon forced the removal of the students to Damascus, Syria.

Since the mid-17th century, the Syrian Patriarchate has included an autonomous church in India, a part of which is now called the "Malankara Syrian Orthodox Church," and headed by Catholicos

Mar Baselios Paulos II (born 1915, elected 1975). See also the Malankara Orthodox Syrian Church: II,E.

The Syrian Orthodox Archdiocese of USA and Canada is headed by Archbishop Mar Athanasius Yeshue Samuel (49 Kipp Avenue, Lodi, New Jersey 07644). It includes 12 Syrian and 11 Malankara parishes in the USA, and four Syrian and one Malankara parishes in Canada. Archbishop Mar Timotheos Aphrem Aboodi is Patriarchal Vicar for Australia (PO Box 257, Lidcombe 2141), where there are six churches.

LOCATION:Syria, Lebanon, Turkey, Israel, India, diaspora
HEAD: Patriarch Ignatius Zakka I Iwas (born 1933, elected 1980)
Title: Syrian Orthodox Patriarch of Antioch and all the East
Residence: Damascus, Syria
MEMBERSHIP: 250,000, plus 1,000,000 in India

## II. E. The Malankara Orthodox Syrian Church

In the mid-17th century, increasingly upset with the latinization of their church by the Portuguese, most of the Thomas Christians in India (see Assyrian Church of the East, I) broke away from the Catholic Church. The leader of the dissidents may have attempted to reestablish communion with the Assyrian Church of the East, but in any case he did not succeed. Then in 1665, the Syrian Patriarch agreed to send a bishop to head the community on the condition that its leader and his followers agree to accept Syrian christology and follow the West Syrian rite. This group was eventually administered as an autonomous church within the Syrian Patriarchate.

However, in 1912 there was a split in the community when a significant section declared itself an autocephalous church and announced the re-establishment of the ancient Catholicosate of the East in India. This was not accepted by those who remained loyal to the Syrian Patriarch. The two sides were reconciled in 1958 when the Indian Supreme Court declared that only the autocephalous Catholicos and bishops in communion with him had legal standing. But in 1975 the Syrian Patriarch excommunicated and deposed the

Catholicos and appointed a rival, an action which resulted in the community splitting yet again.

The precise size of these two communities is extremely difficult to determine, and hotly disputed by the two sides. Many outside observers believe that about half of the Oriental Orthodox in India, who altogether number about 2,000,000, are part of this auto-cephalous church, while the other half makes up an autonomous church under the supervision of the Syrian Orthodox Patriarchate [see above, II.D].

There are two other churches in Kerala which originated in the Malankara Orthodox community. Due in part to the activity of Anglican missionaries, a reform movement grew up within this church in the 19th century. Those who adhered to the movement eventually formed The Mar Thoma Syrian Church of Malabar, which to a great extent conserves oriental liturgical practice and ethos. This church, whose episcopal succession derives from the Syrian Orthodox Church, tends to accept reformed theology, and has been in communion with the Anglican Provinces since 1974. It now has about 700,000 members.

In the late 18th century, a Syrian prelate from Jerusalem ordained a local monk as bishop, but he was not accepted by the Malankara Metropolitan. This bishop then fled to the north and established his own group of followers at the village of Thozhiyoor. Less than 10,000 faithful make up this church today, which is called The Malabar Independent Syrian Church of Thozhiyoor. While preserving its oriental heritage, this group has links with the Mar Thoma Church and increasingly with the Anglican Communion.

The Malankara Orthodox Syrian Church administers the Orthodox Theological Seminary at Kottayam, which was founded in the early 19th century and now has about 75 students. New facilities have recently been built, including the "Sophia Centre" for the training of laymen. The church also operates a number of colleges, schools, hospitals and orphanages.

This church also has a modest monastic tradition. There are four communities of men which follow a monastic rule, and eleven for celibate priests and laity without a definite monastic order. There are also ten convents where nuns live a dedicated life of service and worship.

The Metropolitan of North America is Mar Makarios Thomas (1114 Delaware Avenue, Buffalo, New York 14209). There are 43 priests and 25 parishes within his jurisdiction. In Great Britain contact Fr. K. A. George, 154 Bramley Road, London N14 4HU. There is also a parish in Australia which can be reached through Fr. Skariah at 73 Little George Street, Fitzroy VIC 3065.

LOCATION: India, small diaspora

HEAD: Baselius Mar Thoma Matthews II (born 1915, elected 1991)

Title: Catholicos of the East; Catholicos of the Apostolic Throne of St. Thomas

Residence: Kottayam, Kerala State, India

MEMBERSHIP: 1,000,000

## III. The Orthodox Church

Orthodox Christians consider themselves to be one church in the sense that they share the same faith and sacraments, as well as the Byzantine liturgical, canonical, and spiritual tradition. All Orthodox recognize the first seven ecumenical councils as normative for doctrine and church life. A number of later councils are also considered to reflect the same original faith. Although referred to most commonly as The Orthodox Church, this communion is also frequently called the Eastern Orthodox Church to distinguish it from the Oriental Orthodox Churches described in the previous section.

At the level of church government, Orthodoxy is a communion of churches, all of which recognize the Patriarch of Constantinople as "first among equals." Although he does not have authority to intervene in the affairs of local churches outside his own patriarchate, he is considered first in honor, and the symbolic center of all the Orthodox churches. Thus the Patriarchate of Constantinople (also known as the Ecumenical Patriarchate) enjoys a certain "priority" among the various Orthodox Churches. It sees this status as a service which provides a mechanism for the functioning of conciliarity and mutual responsibility among the Orthodox Churches. This role includes convoking the churches and coordinating their activity, and at times intervening in situations in view of finding solutions to specific problems.

The schism between what are now known as the Orthodox and Catholic Churches was the result of a centuries-long process of estrangement between the two communions. Such events as the excommunications of 1054 between the Patriarch of Constantinople and the papal legate were only high points in this process. Moreover, each Orthodox Church has its own history concerning the rift with Rome. There was, for example, never a formal separation between Rome and the Patriarchate of Antioch, although Antioch came to share the common Byzantine perception of the schism. Today it is widely agreed that there were significant non-theological factors at play in this gradual alienation between east and west. These included the cutting off of ordinary contact imposed by political developments, and the loss of the ability to understand the Greek or Latin of the other church. But doctrinal issues were also involved, especially in relation to divergent understandings of the nature of the Church. The most important of these concerned the eternal procession of the Holy Spirit (related to the addition of the *filioque* to the Creed by the western church), and the meaning of the bishop of Rome's position as first bishop in the Church.

Two major attempts to reestablish communion between Catholics and Orthodox took place at the Second Council of Lyons in 1274 and the Council of Ferrara-Florence in 1438-9. Although formal reunions were proclaimed in both cases, they were ultimately rejected by the general Orthodox population. Many centuries of mutual isolation have been ended only in the contemporary period. An official international dialogue between the two churches has been in progress since 1980.

## III. A. The Autocephalous Orthodox Churches

Today there are thirteen Orthodox churches which are generally accepted to be "autocephalous," which in Greek literally means "self-headed." An autocephalous church possesses the right to resolve all internal problems on its own authority, and the ability to choose its own bishops, including the Patriarch or Metropolitan who heads the church. While each acts independently, they all remain in full sacramental and canonical communion with one another. These autocephalous Orthodox churches include the four ancient eastern patriarchates (Constantinople, Alexandria, Antioch, and Jerusalem), and nine other Orthodox churches which have emerged over the centuries.

There is not, however, unanimous agreement about which churches possess autocephalous status. The Patriarchate of Constantinople claims the exclusive right to grant autocephaly. It and most other Orthodox Churches recognize, in addition to the four ancient patriarchates, the churches of Russia, Serbia, Romania, Bulgaria, Georgia, Cyprus, Greece, Poland, and Albania as having this rank. But the Patriarchate of Moscow has, on its own initiative, granted autocephalous status to the Orthodox Church in what are now the Czech and Slovak Republics, and to most of its parishes in North America under the name of the Orthodox Church in America.

Nine of these autocephalous churches are Patriarchates: Constantinople, Alexandria, Antioch, Jerusalem, Russia, Serbia, Romania, Bulgaria and Georgia. The others are headed by an Archbishop or Metropolitan.

## III. A. 1. The Patriarchate of Constantinople

In New Testament times, Greek culture was predominant in the eastern regions of the Roman Empire. The early growth of the Church, beginning with the missionary activity of St. Paul, eventually led to the full Christianization of this Greek civilization.

The Emperor Constantine began a process which led to the adoption of Christianity as the imperial state religion by Emperor Theodosius in the late 4th century. Constantine also moved the empire's capital from Rome to the small Greek city of Byzantium in 330 and renamed it Constantinople, or New Rome. The church in ancient Rome, however, was still considered the first of the local churches, followed by Alexandria and Antioch.

But because of its new status as capital of the empire, the church of the imperial capital grew in importance. Canon 3 of the First Council of Constantinople stated that the bishop of that city had a precedence of honor just after the Bishop of Rome because it is the New Rome. And in its disputed 28th Canon, the Council of Chalcedon in 451 recognized an expansion of the boundaries of the Patriarchate of Constantinople, and its authority over bishops of dioceses "among the barbarians" — which has been variously interpreted as meaning either areas outside the Byzantine Empire, or among non-Greeks. In any case, for almost a thousand years the Patriarch of Constantinople presided over the church in the eastern

Roman (Byzantine) Empire, and its missionary activity which brought the Christian faith in its Byzantine form to many peoples north of the imperial borders. The cathedral church of Constantinople, Hagia Sophia (Holy Wisdom), was the center of religious life in the eastern Christian world.

The schism between Rome and Constantinople developed over a long period, and is often described in older books as culminating in 1054 with the mutual excommunications between the Patriarch Michael Cerularius and Cardinal Humbert, the papal legate. But for the common people in the Empire, the rift took on real meaning only after the 1204 sacking of Constantinople by the Latins during the fourth crusade.

Even though Constantinople fell to the Turks in 1453, the Patriarch remained the head of the multi-ethnic Orthodox communities within the Turkish (Ottoman) Empire, and retained his position as the first Orthodox patriarch. This gave him a certain authority over the Greek Patriarchates of Alexandria, Antioch, and Jerusalem which were also within Ottoman territory.

In the 19th century, an independent Greek state was established, with its own autocephalous church. After World War I, there was a major exchange of populations between Greece and Turkey. Anti-Greek riots in Istanbul (the new Turkish name for Constantinople) in the 1950's precipitated another exodus of Greeks from Turkey. Now very few remain.

Today the Patriarchate of Constantinople includes the 4,000 to 5,000 Greeks who remain in Turkey, as well as some sections of Greece (Mount Athos, the semi-autonomous Church of Crete, and the Dodecanese Islands). There was an important theological school on the island of Halki, near Istanbul, until it was closed by the government in 1971. The present Patriarch has given high priority to the re-opening of the Halki school. The Patriarchate administers certain theological academic institutions in Greece, including a school at the monastery of John the Theologian on Patmos, the Patriarchal Institute for Patristic Studies in Thessalonika, and the Orthodox Academy of Crete. It also maintains an Orthodox Center at Chambésy, Switzerland, near Geneva. In December 1989 the

Patriarchate inaugurated a new administrative headquarters at the Phanar, replacing the original 17th-century building which had been destroyed in a fire in 1941. It was only in 1987 that the Turkish government had granted permission to rebuild the edifice.

The Greek Orthodox in the diaspora are part of the Ecumenical Patriarchate, as well as a number of other jurisdictions of various ethnic backgrounds [see section III.C below]. Archbishop Gregorios of Thyateira and Great Britain has offices at Thyateira House, 5 Craven Hill, W2 3EN London. There are 76 places of worship in Britain, and one parish in Dublin, Ireland.

Archbishop Stylianos presides over Greek Orthodox faithful in Australia (242 Cleveland Street, Redfern, Sydney, NSW 2016). The Australian Archdiocese, which includes 121 parishes, has recently opened St. Andrew's Greek Orthodox Theological College in Sydney. Greek Orthodox in New Zealand (5 parishes) and large parts of Asia are under the pastoral care of Metropolitan Dionysios (P.O. Box 9361, Courtenay Pl., Wellington, N.Z.).

The Greek Orthodox Archdiocese of North and South America is presided over by Archbishop Iakovos (10 East 79th Street, New York, N.Y. 10021). In the USA there are eight dioceses, and 509 parishes. Canadian Greek Orthodox have 68 parishes within the Diocese of Toronto, under the guidance of Bishop Sotirios (40 Donlands Avenue, Toronto, Ontario M4J 3N6). The Archdiocese of North and South America administers Hellenic College/Holy Cross Greek Orthodox School of Theology in Brookline, Massachusetts.

LOCATION: Turkey, Greece, the Americas, Western Europe, Australia

HEAD: Patriarch Bartholomew I (born 1940, elected 1991)

Title: Archbishop of Constantinople/New Rome, Ecumenical Patriarch

Residence: Istanbul (Constantinople), Turkey

MEMBERSHIP: 3,500,000

## III. A. 2. The Patriarchate of Alexandria

Until the period following the Council of Chalcedon (451 A.D.), the Christians in Egypt were united in a single Patriarchate. The controversy surrounding Chalcedon's christological teaching, however, led to a split between the majority which rejected the Council [The Coptic Orthodox Church: see II.B], and the largely Greek minority which accepted it. The Greek Orthodox Patriarchate of Alexandria is descended from the latter group. By the 7th century, it has been estimated that there were 17 or 18 million Copts in Egypt, and approximately 200,000 (mostly imperial officials, soldiers, merchants and other Greeks) who accepted Chalcedon. At this time both groups used the ancient Alexandrian liturgy, but in the Greek Patriarchate it was gradually replaced by the Byzantine liturgy, the Alexandrian rite having died out by the 12th century.

With the Arab conquest of Egypt in 638, the Greeks in the area suffered persecution because of their links with the Byzantine Empire. This difficult situation became even worse with the Turkish conquest of Egypt in 1517, after which the Greek Patriarchs of Alexandria usually lived in Constantinople. For a long period there were no resident Greek Orthodox bishops in Egypt. Only in 1846, with the election of Patriarch Hierothios, were the Patriarchs able to reside in Alexandria again.

In the early years of the 20th century, a significant immigration of Greeks and Orthodox Arabs into Egypt and other parts of Africa increased the membership of the Patriarchate. Today the Patriarchate has jurisdiction over all the Orthodox faithful in Africa, who are mostly Greeks.

In the 1930's a spontaneous movement of indigenous Africans towards the Orthodox Church began in Uganda under the leadership of a former Anglican, Reuben Spartas. He was received into full communion with the Greek Orthodox Patriarchate in 1946, and the Orthodox communities in East Africa that had been founded under his leadership were organized into the Archdiocese of Irinoupolis with headquarters in Nairobi in 1958. This group is now served by a growing native African clergy, including three bishops and about 150 priests. There are 113 parishes in Kenya, 29 in Uganda, and nine in Tanzania.

The Archbishop Makarios III of Cyprus Patriarchal Orthodox Seminary, located in Nairobi, Kenya, had 30 students in 1992 from East Africa. There are two male religious communities in Cairo and one in Alexandria.

LOCATION: Egypt, the rest of Africa.

HEAD: Pope Parthenios III (born 1919, elected 1987)

Title: Pope and Patriarch of Alexandria and All Africa

Residence: Alexandria, Egypt.

MEMBERSHIP: 350,000

## III. A. 3. The Patriarchate of Antioch

Antioch was a very important urban center in the ancient world, and it was there, according to the Book of Acts, that the followers of Jesus were first called Christians. Antioch eventually became the seat of a Patriarchate which included all the Christians in the vast Eastern Province of the Roman Empire and beyond.

But the Council of Chalcedon triggered a schism in the Patriarchate. The larger group, which repudiated the Council, eventually formed the Syrian Orthodox Church [see II.D]. This church is made up of those who accepted Chalcedon, mostly Greeks and hellenized sections of the indigenous population.

Such was the situation when Antioch fell to the Arab invaders in August 638. Perceived as allies of the Byzantine enemy, the local Greeks now underwent a long period of persecution, and the Patriarchal throne was often vacant or occupied by a non-resident bishop during the 7th and first half of the 8th centuries.

The Byzantines regained possession of the city in 969, and until 1085, when Antioch fell to the Seljuk Turks, the Greek Patriarchate prospered under Byzantine rule. During this period, the West Syrian liturgy was gradually replaced by the Byzantine liturgy, a process which would be complete by the 12th century.

In 1098, the Crusaders took Antioch and set up a Latin kingdom in Syria which would last nearly two centuries. A Latin Patriarchate of Antioch was established, while a line of Greek Patriarchs continued in exile.

After Antioch was taken by the Egyptian Mamelukes in 1268, the Greek Patriarch was able to return to the area. Because Antioch itself had long ago been reduced to a small town, the patriarchate was permanently transferred to Damascus in the 14th century. The area was taken from the Mamelukes by the Ottoman Turks in 1517, and remained under Turkish control until the end of World War I.

By this time the great majority of the faithful of this patriarchate were Arabs. In 1898 the last Greek Patriarch was deposed, and an Arab successor was elected in 1899. Thus the patriarchate became fully Arab in character.

A strong renewal movement, involving Orthodox youth in particular, has been under way since the 1940's. The present Patriarch has been active in the ecumenical movement, and has been participating in efforts to reestablish the unity of all those whose roots can be traced back to the ancient undivided Antioch Patriarchate.

The St. John of Damascus Academy of Theology, located near Tripoli, Lebanon, was established by the patriarchate in 1970. In 1988 it was officially incorporated into Balamand University.

There has been extensive immigration to the new world in recent years, and dioceses have been established in North America, Argentina, and Brazil. In North America the Antiochian Orthodox Christian Archdiocese is under the supervision of Metropolitan Philip Saliba (358 Mountain Road, Englewood, New Jersey 07631). The Archdiocese has 145 parishes in the USA and 12 in Canada. This jurisdiction includes a number of "Western Rite" parishes of Episcopalian (Anglican) origin, as well as a distinct "Antiochian Evangelical Orthodox Mission," which originated in the Campus Crusade for Christ.

The Australian Antiochian Orthodox Diocese is headed by Bishop Gibran of Larissa (Box 120, Randwick, NSW 2031), and has 4 parishes. London, England, is also host to one Antiochian Orthodox worshiping community.

LOCATION: Lebanon, Syria, Iraq, Iran, the Americas, Australia
HEAD: Patriarch Ignatius IV (born 1920, elected 1979)
Title: Patriarch of Antioch and All the East
Residence: Damascus, Syria
MEMBERSHIP: 750,000

## III. A. 4. The Patriarchate of Jerusalem

Given its association with the life of Jesus, Jerusalem has always been of great importance for Christians. As the Christian faith gained wider acceptance in the Roman Empire, the prestige of Jerusalem grew as well. The Emperor Constantine, who was very favorable to Christianity, caused magnificent basilicas to be built over some of the holy places in the 4th century. Monasticism had come to Palestine very soon after the first Christian communities were founded in Egypt, and monasteries continued to flourish in the area, especially in the desert between Jerusalem and the Dead Sea.

At the Council of Chalcedon in 451, it was decided to raise the Church of Jerusalem to the rank of Patriarchate. In doing so, three ecclesiastical provinces with about sixty dioceses were detached from the Patriarchate of Antioch, to which the area had previously belonged. Under Greek Byzantine rule, Jerusalem continued to thrive as the destination of countless Christian pilgrims.

But this prosperity was brought to an end by the invasions of the Persians in 614 and the Arabs in 637. Most Christian churches and monasteries were destroyed, and much of the population gradually converted to Islam.

In 1099 Jerusalem was taken by the Crusaders who established a kingdom which would endure for almost a century. During this period a Latin Patriarchate of Jerusalem was established, while a line of Greek Patriarchs continued in exile, usually residing in Constantinople. The Greek Patriarchs began living at or near Jerusalem again following the collapse of the Crusader kingdom.

Jerusalem fell to the Seljuk Turks in 1187, but was soon taken by the Egyptian Mamelukes. The Ottoman Turks gained control of the city in 1516. During the 400 years of Ottoman rule there were many struggles between Christian groups over possession of the holy places. In the mid-19th century, the Turks confirmed Greek control over most of them. This arrangement has remained unchanged during the British mandate which began in 1917, and under subsequent Jordanian and Israeli administrations.

The fact that the hierarchy of the Patriarchate is Greek while the faithful are Arab has been a source of contention in recent times. The patriarch and bishops are drawn from the Brotherhood of the Holy Sepulcher, a Jerusalem Greek monastic community founded in the 16th century. The married clergy, however, are from the local Arab population. The longstanding tensions resulting from this situation came into the open once again in 1992. A new organization, the Arab Orthodox Initiative Committee, began to press for Arab participation in the Patriarchate's financial decisions, and, over the long term, for the Arabization of the church. These efforts, however, were being vigorously resisted by Patriarch Diodoros and the Holy Synod, who asserted the historically Greek character of the Patriarchate.

The Jerusalem Patriarchate has also taken a negative stance towards the ecumenical movement: in 1989 it withdrew its delegates from all the bilateral dialogues in which the Orthodox Church is currently engaged. The Patriarch stated that other Christians were using the dialogues as a means of proselytism, and that, since the Orthodox Church already possesses the fullness of Christian truth, it had no need to participate in such discussions.

The Byzantine liturgy is celebrated in Greek in the monasteries but in Arabic in the parishes. A Greek Orthodox College is maintained in Jerusalem, and there are schools in many of the parishes.

LOCATION: Israel and Jordan

HEAD: Patriarch Diodoros I (born 1923, elected 1981)

Title: The Greek Orthodox Patriarch of Jerusalem

Residence: Jerusalem

MEMBERSHIP: 260,000

## III. A. 5. The Orthodox Church of Russia

In the late 10th century, according to the legend, the pagan Grand Prince Vladimir of Kiev sent envoys to different parts of the world to examine the local religions and to advise him which would be best for his kingdom. When the envoys returned, they recommended the faith of the Greeks, for they reported that when they attended the divine liturgy in the cathedral of Hagia Sophia in Constantinople, "we did not know if we were in heaven or on earth." After the baptism of Prince Vladimir, many of his followers were baptized in the waters of the Dnieper river in 988. Thus Byzantine Christianity became the faith of the three peoples who trace their origins to Rus' of Kiev: the Ukrainians, Belarusians, and Russians.

Christian Kiev flourished for a time, but then entered a period of decline which culminated in 1240 when the city was destroyed during the Mongol invasions. As a result of the Mongol destruction, large numbers of people moved northward. By the 14th century a new center grew up around the principality of Moscow, and the Metropolitans of Kiev took up residence there. Later, Moscow was declared the metropolitan see in its own right.

When Constantinople fell to the Turks in 1453, Russia was throwing off Mongol rule and becoming an independent state. Because the first Rome was said to have fallen into heresy and the New Rome had fallen under the Turks, some Russians began to speak of Moscow as the "Third Rome" which would carry on the traditions of Orthodoxy and Roman civilization. The czar (caesar) was now the champion and protector of Orthodoxy just as the Byzantine Emperor once had been. The Russian Church had already begun to develop its own style of iconography and church architecture, and its own theological and spiritual traditions.

In the mid-17th century a schism took place in this church when Patriarch Nikon reformed a number of Russian liturgical usages to make them conform with those of the Greek church. Those who refused to submit to the reform, and insisted on continuing these uniquely Russian traditions, came to be known as "Old Believers." [see III.D.1]

A Russian Orthodox Patriarchate was officially established by Constantinople in 1589, but it was abolished by Peter the Great in 1721. The church was then administered by a Holy Synod under regulations which brought the church under close state supervision. During this period, especially in the 19th century, a great revival of Russian Orthodox theology, spirituality, and monasticism took place.

In August 1917, after the abdication of the czar but before the Bolshevik Revolution, a synod of the Russian Orthodox Church began in Moscow. It reestablished the Russian Patriarchate and elected Tikhon as Patriarch of Moscow. But before the synod ended, it was learned that the Metropolitan of Kiev had been murdered, and that persecutions had begun. Patriarch Tikhon was outspoken in his criticism of the communists in his early years as patriarch, but moderated his publicly expressed views after a year in prison.

Although there were periods of greater or lesser persecution after 1917, the *modus vivendi* worked out under Patriarch Tikhon and his successor Patriarch Sergei remained basically the same under communism: the Russian Orthodox Church publicly supported the government on all issues, and the government in turn reduced its persecution. In practice, church activity was restricted to liturgical worship.

Many churches were closed after the revolution, and another massive wave of church closings took place under Khrushchev in 1960-1963. In 1914, 54,457 churches were registered, but in the late 1970's there were less than 7,000. The number of functioning monasteries (1,498 in 1914) was down to 12, and the 57 theological seminaries operating in 1914 had been reduced to three in Moscow, Leningrad, and Odessa, with theological academies of higher studies in the first two cities.

After 1990, however, thanks to the reforms set in motion by President Mikhail Gorbachev, the situation of the Russian Orthodox Church began to improve dramatically. Metropolitan Kyrill of Smolensk reported in the summer of 1992 that the number of parishes had risen to about 14,000 and the number of monasteries to 149. His church now had eight seminaries and three theological academies (Moscow, St. Petersburg and Kiev), as well as twenty theological colleges which were providing rapid preparation for ordination. In addition, in October 1992 the Saint Tikhon of Moscow Theological Institute was opened in Moscow for training the Orthodox laity. The students, more or less evenly divided between women and men, numbered some 650 in the first year. And on February 24, 1993, the first Russian Orthodox university in history, named after St. John the Theologian, opened in Moscow.

The gradual disintegration of the communist system and the Soviet Union created centrifugal forces which threatened the unity of the Moscow Patriarchate. In January 1990, when conditions were already improving, the Bishops' Council of the Russian Orthodox Church met in Moscow and decided to grant a certain measure of autonomy to the Orthodox Churches in Ukraine and Byelorussia (now Belarus). Each of these were made Exarchates of the Moscow Patriarchate, with the optional names "The Ukrainian Orthodox Church" and "The Byelorussian (now Belarusian) Orthodox Church." Following the dissolution of the Soviet Union on December 25, 1991, and the independence of the various successor states, the Patriarchate granted similar autonomous status to the Orthodox churches in Estonia, Latvia and Moldova.

But because the Orthodox Church in Ukraine was demanding greater freedom, on 27 October 1990, another session of the Bishops' Council granted "independence and self-government" to the Ukrainian Orthodox Church, and abolished the title "Ukrainian Exarchate." Even so, the church remained only autonomous, with the Metropolitan of Kiev still a member of the Holy Synod of the Moscow Patriarchate. After Ukraine declared its independence on 24 August 1991, Metropolitan Filaret of Kiev began to seek full auto-cephalous status from Moscow. This, however, was refused at a meeting of the Bishop's Council in April 1992. Matters came to a head in May 1992 when the Moscow Patriarchate deposed Filaret and appointed Metropolitan Volodymyr (Sabodan) of Rostov as new Metropolitan of Kiev. In June the Patriarchate defrocked Filaret and reduced him to the lay state. Subsequently Filaret joined the non-canonical Ukrainian Autocephalous Church [see III.D.3]. As of this writing this autonomous church linked to Moscow was still the largest of the Orthodox churches in Ukraine.

There was another problem in the newly-independent republic of Moldova which (then known as Bessarabia) had been a part of Romania before 1812 and again from 1918 to 1944. In spite of the fact that the Moscow Patriarchate had granted it autonomous status, the Holy Synod of the Romanian Orthodox Church decided in December 1992 to reconstitute its own Metropolitanate of Bessarabia in the same country. Thus the Orthodox in Moldova are now split between the two rival jurisdictions.

And in Estonia, while work was proceeding in early 1993 on the elaboration of a new statute regulating the autonomous status of the Orthodox Church there, a group calling itself the Estonian Orthodox Church met in Tallinn in April for the first time since the end of communist rule. This group called for the reestablishment of the autonomous Orthodox Church of Estonia under the Patriarchate of Constantinople that had existed in the country from 1923 until Soviet annexation in World War II.

The parishes in North America under the Moscow Patriarchate are administered by Bishop Pavel Ponomarjov of Zaraisk (15 East 97th Street, New York, New York 10029). The 25 Patriarchal parishes in Canada are in Alberta and Saskatchewan. The Patriarchate's 20 places of worship in Britain are presided over by Metropolitan Anthony Bloom of Sourozh (67 Ennismore Gardens, London SW7 1NH). Moscow has also recently established two parishes in Australia. Contact Fr. Peter Hill, Glen Iris Road, Glen Iris VIC 3146.

See also the Orthodox Church in America [III.A.15], the Russian Orthodox Archdiocese in Western Europe [III.C.3], and the Russian Orthodox Church Outside Russia [III.D.2].

Location: Russia and the other countries of the Commonwealth of Independent States, diaspora

HEAD: Patriarch Aleksy II (born 1929, elected 1990)

Title: Patriarch of Moscow and All Russia

Residence: Moscow, Russia

MEMBERSHIP: 50,000,000

## III. A. 6. The Orthodox Church of Serbia

The origins of Christianity in Serbia are obscure. It is known that Latin missionaries were active along the Dalmatian coast in the 7th century, and that by the 9th century Byzantine missionaries were at work in Serbia, having been sent by Emperor Basil I the Macedonian. Eventually the Serbian people became entirely Christian.

Due in part to its geographical location, the Serbian Church vacillated between Rome and Constantinople for a time, but finally gravitated towards the Byzantines. In 1219, St. Sava was consecrated the first Archbishop of a self-governing Serbian Orthodox Church by the Patriarch of Constantinople, then residing at Nicaea during the Latin occupation of his city.

The Serbian kingdom reached its apogee during the reign of Stevan Dushan, who extended Serbian rule to Albania, Thessaly, Epirus, and Macedonia. Dushan was crowned Emperor of the Serbians and established a Serbian Patriarchate at Peč in 1346. This state of affairs was recognized by Constantinople in 1375.

The Serbians were defeated by the Turks in 1389, and subsequently they were gradually integrated into the Ottoman Empire. The Serbian Patriarchate was suppressed by the Turks in 1459, only to be restored by them in 1557. But it was suppressed again in 1766, as the Greek Patriarch was asserting his role as head of all Orthodox under Turkish rule.

The emergence of an independent Serbian state in 1830 was coupled with recognition of the autonomy of the Orthodox metropolia based at Belgrade, and in 1879 the Patriarch of Constantinople recognized the Serbian Church as autocephalous. In 1918 the multinational state of Yugoslavia was formed. This made possible the amalgamation of various Orthodox jurisdictions now within Yugoslavia (the formerly autonomous Serbian metropolia of Belgrade, Karlovči, Bosnia, Montenegro, and the diocese of Dalmatia) into a single Serbian Orthodox Church. In 1920 this union was recognized by Constantinople and raised to the rank of Patriarchate.

The Serbian church suffered heavily during World War II, especially in regions under the control of the fascist independent

Croatian state. Altogether it lost some 25% of its churches and monasteries, and about one fifth of its clergy. Following the
establishment of a communist Yugoslav government in 1945, the
Serbian church had to work out a new relationship with the state.
But Tito's break with the Soviet Union in 1948 and development of
better relations with the West led to greater tolerance of religion and
an improved situation for the church. Nevertheless, subtle forms of
persecution continued, with the government supporting a schism
within the Serbian Orthodox Church [see the Macedonian Orthodox
Church, III.D.5].

Following the breakup of Yugoslavia into various republics, the
Serbian Orthodox Church became more involved in political matters.
In May 1992 it began to distance itself from the Milosevic regime and
called for a government of national unity. But it also vigorously
supported the efforts of Serbian minorities in Croatia and Bosnia-
Herzegovina to achieve political union with Serbia itself.

The highest authority in the Serbian Church is the Holy Assembly
of Bishops, composed of all the diocesan bishops. But the Holy
Synod of Bishops, made up of the Patriarch and four bishops, gov-
erns the church on a day-to-day basis. There is a theological institute
in Belgrade (founded 1921), four seminaries, and a school for the
training of monks. Fifteen religious publications are sponsored by
the Patriarchate and other dioceses.

A Serbian Orthodox Diocese of North America was formed in
1913. But the American community experienced a split in 1963 over
the relationship between the Serbian Patriarchate and the communist
Yugoslav government. Those who felt the relationship was tanta-
mount to collaboration formed the "Free Serbian Orthodox Church,"
later known as the "New Gracanica Metropolitanate," and broke all
canonical links with Belgrade. It was only in 1991 that there was a
reconciliation between the two groups under Patriarch Pavle, although for the time being the ecclesiastical structures of both will
continue to exist.

The New Gracanica jurisdiction is headed by Metropolitan Ireney
(P.O. Box 371, Grayslake, Illinois 60030). The North American dioceses which had remained part of the Serbian Patriarchate are

presided over by Metropolitan Christopher (St. Sava Monastery, Box 519, Libertyville, Illinois 60048). The diocese of Canada is under the pastoral care of Bishop George (5a Stockbridge Avenue, Toronto Ontario M8Z 4M6). Altogether there are 52 parishes in the US and 10 in Canada. In addition, Bishop Luka presides over 17 parishes in Australia and New Zealand from St. Sava Monastery, Mt. Mercer Road, Elaine, Victoria 3334. In Britain there are 22 Serbian Orthodox worshiping communities under the jurisdiction of Bishop Dositej in Sweden.

> Location: Yugoslavia and former republics, Western Europe, North America, Australia
>
> HEAD: Patriarch Pavle I (born 1914, elected 1990)
>
> Title: Archbishop of Peč, Metropolitan of Belgrade and Karlovči, Patriarch of the Serbians.
>
> Residence: Belgrade, Yugoslavia
>
> MEMBERSHIP: 8,000,000

## III. A. 7. The Orthodox Church of Romania

The Romanian Orthodox Church is unique among the Orthodox Churches because it alone exists within a Latin culture. Romanian is a romance tongue, directly descended from the language of the Roman soldiers and settlers who occupied Dacia and intermarried with its inhabitants following its conquest by Emperor Trajan in 106 AD.

Christianity in the area has been traced back to apostolic times, but the history of its development during the millennium following the withdrawal of Roman administration in 271 is obscure. Certainly both Latin and Byzantine missionaries had been active in the area. In any case, by the time the Romanian principalities of Moldavia and Wallachia emerged as political entities in the 14th century, Romanian ethnic identity was already closely identified with the Orthodox Christian faith. Approval was given for the liturgy to be celebrated in Romanian at a local synod in 1568.

The following centuries witnessed the development of a distinct Romanian theological tradition in spite of the fact that Wallachia and Moldavia were vassals of the Ottoman Empire from the 16th to the 19th centuries. The two principalities were united under a single prince in 1859, and Romania gained full independence in 1878. Consequently, the Patriarchate of Constantinople, which had exercised jurisdiction over the Romanians while they were within the Ottoman Empire, recognized the autocephalous status of the Romanian Church in 1885. Transylvania, which included large numbers of Orthodox Romanians, was integrated into the Romanian kingdom after World War I, and the Romanian Church was raised to the rank of Patriarchate in 1925.

The establishment of a communist government in Romania after World War II required a new *modus vivendi* between church and state. In general, the Romanian Orthodox Church adopted a policy of close cooperation with the government. Whatever the merits of that decision may have been, the church was able to maintain an active and meaningful existence in the country. A strong spiritual renewal movement took place in the 1950's. A large number of churches were left open, and there were many functioning monasteries, although all church activity was kept under strict government supervision. There were six seminaries and two theological institutes (in Sibiu and Bucharest). High quality theological journals were published, including three by the Patriarchate itself and one by each of the five metropolitanates, and important theological works as well.

Following the overthrow of the government of Nicolae Ceauşescu in December 1989, the Romanian Orthodox hierarchy was severely criticized from many quarters for having cooperated with the communist regime. Patriarch Teoctist resigned his office in January 1990, but was reinstated by the Holy Synod the following April. Since that time, however, the Romanian Orthodox Church seems to have stabilized its position and is experiencing a sustained growth in its activity.

As of early 1993 no less than 18 seminaries were functioning, where nuns and laypeople could also study basic theology. Higher studies in theology are now integrated into the state university system, where there are 12 faculties of Orthodox theology around the country. Monastic life is thriving in 192 monasteries and 75 sketes. There has also been a proliferation of theological journals and newspapers.

In 1993 the Romanian Patriarchate reestablished jurisdictions in areas which were part of Romanian territory in the interwar period: in northern Bukovina (now in Ukraine) and Bessarabia, most of which is now the independent republic of Moldova. The Orthodox Church in Moldova had been part of the Russian Orthodox Church since World War II, and had just been granted autonomous status by Moscow. Thus Moldovan Orthodox faithful were divided between the two competing jurisdictions.

The Romanian Patriarchate has a diocese in North America headed by Archbishop Victorin Ursache (Romanian Orthodox Missionary Episcopate of America, 19959 Riopelle Avenue, Detroit, Michigan 48203). It has 13 parishes in the USA and 21 in Canada. Romanian Orthodox in Britain are cared for by Fr. P. Pufulete at 8, Elsynge Road, Battersea London SW 18. The community in Australia, which has five parishes, can be contacted through Fr. Gabriel Popescu, PO Box 558, Campsie NSW 2194. Metropolitan Nicolae Corneanu of Banat has been named by the Holy Synod as Exarch for all Orthodox Romanians in the diaspora.

Another Romanian Orthodox jurisdiction is part of the Orthodox Church in America [see III.A.15]. It is presided over by Bishop Nathaniel Popp (Romanian Orthodox Episcopate of the Americas, Vatra Româneasca, 2522 Grey Tower Road, Jackson, Michigan 49201). There are 41 parishes in the USA and 16 in Canada.

Location: Romania, diaspora in western Europe and North America

HEAD: Patriarch Teoctist I (born 1915, elected 1986)

Title: Archbishop of Bucharest, Metropolitan of Ungro-Wallachia, Patriarch of the Romanian Orthodox Church

Residence: Bucharest, Romania

MEMBERSHIP: 19,800,000

## *III. A. 8. The Orthodox Church of Bulgaria*

A Christian presence in the territory of modern Bulgaria can be traced back to early centuries, as a council of bishops met in Sardica (now Sofia) in 343. The region was subsequently occupied by Bulgar tribes who, although pagan, had already had some contacts with Christian missionaries. The decisive moment in the development of Christianity among the Bulgarians was the baptism of King Boris I by a Byzantine bishop in 865, which was followed by the gradual Christianization of the Bulgarian people. Bulgaria wavered between Rome and Constantinople for a time and became the subject of a major dispute between the two churches. But in the end Bulgaria opted for Constantinople and Byzantine civilization.

The Bulgarian state became very powerful in the 10th century. In 927 Constantinople recognized the king as Emperor of the Bulgarians and the Archbishop of Preslav as Patriarch of the Bulgarian Church. But the Byzantines gained strength and invaded the Bulgarian Empire in 971, at which time the Patriarch left Preslav and took up residence at Ohrid, Macedonia. The Byzantines conquered Macedonia in 1018, and reduced the patriarchate to the rank of autocephalous archbishopric.

Bulgaria regained its independence in 1186 with the establishment of the second empire based at Turnovo. After lengthy negotiations the Bulgarian Church recognized the supremacy of the Pope in 1204. But this agreement ended in 1235 when the Bulgarian Emperor. made an alliance with the Greeks against the Latin Empire in Constantinople, and the Byzantine patriarch recognized a second Bulgarian Orthodox patriarchate in return.

With the beginning of Turkish domination in 1393, the Bulgarian Church lost its autocephalous character and was integrated into the Patriarchate of Constantinople. In 1870 the Ottoman government allowed the reestablishment of a national Bulgarian Church as an autonomous exarchate. Constantinople reacted strongly and declared the Bulgarian Church schismatic in 1872. This rift continued long after Bulgaria became a principality in 1878 and an independent kingdom in 1908. It was only in 1945 that the Ecumenical

Patriarchate recognized the Bulgarian Church as autocephalous and ended the schism. The Metropolitan of Sofia assumed the title of Patriarch in 1953 and he was recognized as such by Constantinople in 1961. During the period of communist rule, which began in 1944, the government followed a religious policy similar to that of the Soviet Union, and the church was compelled to play a largely passive role in society.

Now that the communist system has collapsed, the Bulgarian Orthodox Church has had difficulty adapting to the new situation in the country. In 1991 the new government created a Board of Religious Affairs which began to initiate reforms in the country's religious institutions. In March 1992 it ruled that the 1971 election of Patriarch Maxim had been illegal because he had been appointed by the communist government in an uncanonical manner. This triggered a division in the synod of bishops, with three of them publicly calling for Maxim's deposition. In January 1993 a delegation from the Ecumenical Patriarchate visited Sofia to try to facilitate a solution, but without success. At that time the prime minister admitted that the attempt to unseat Maxim had been a mistake. As of spring 1993 Maxim was still recognized as Patriarch by the other Orthodox Churches, and a local council of the Bulgarian Orthodox Church was being planned in the hope of achieving a reconciliation between the two groups.

The Bulgarian Orthodox Holy Synod, made up of the Patriarch and diocesan bishops, meets twice a year and is the highest decision-making body. A Council of Bishops, composed of the Patriarch and four other bishops elected to four-year terms, meets almost continually and deals with current church affairs.

New theology faculties have been created since the fall of communism. At present there are Bulgarian Orthodox seminaries in Plodiv and Sofia, and faculties of theology at the University of Sofia and at St. Cyril and Methodius University in Veliko Tarnovo. In addition, there are 123 functioning monasteries with 400 monks and nuns.

Metropolitan Joseph of America, Canada and Australia resides at 550-A West 50th Street, New York, New York 10019. Altogether there are 23 parishes in the USA, and two in Canada. The community in Australia can be reached through Fr. Todor Popoff at Saint Petka Church, 1 Merlin Road, Fulham Gardens, SA 5024. Bulgarian Orthodox in Britain can be contacted through Fr. Simeon Spassov Iliev, 24 Queen's Gate Gardens, London SW7.

Another Bulgarian Orthodox diocese is part of the Orthodox Church in America [III.A.15]. It is presided over by Bishop Kyrill, whose address is 519 Brynhaven Drive, Toledo, Ohio 43616. There are 13 parishes in the USA and three in Canada.

LOCATION: Bulgaria, small diaspora in Europe and America.
HEAD: Patriarch Maxim (born 1914, elected 1971)
Title: Metropolitan of Sofia, Patriarch of All Bulgaria
Residence: Sofia, Bulgaria
MEMBERSHIP: 8,000,000

## III. A. 9. The Orthodox Church of Georgia

Georgia, which is centered in the Caucasus mountains at the eastern end of the Black Sea, has a civilization which reaches back to ancient times. Due in large part to the missionary activity of St. Nino, a slave girl from Cappadocia, the kingdom of Iberia (East Georgia) adopted the Christian faith as its state religion in 337. West Georgia, then a part of the Roman Empire, became Christian through a gradual process which was virtually complete by the 5th century.

The Jerusalem liturgy of St. James was celebrated in Iberia, at first in Greek, but in Georgian by the 6th century. The Byzantine liturgy was always used in West Georgia, changing from Greek to Georgian in the 8th or 9th century. East Georgia adopted the Byzantine liturgy soon after East and West Georgia were combined into a single kingdom and Catholicosate in 1008.

The Church in Iberia was at first dependent on the Patriarchate of Antioch, but it was established as an independent church by King Vakhtang Gorgaslan in 467. For a time following the Council of Chalcedon (451), the Georgians of Iberia joined the neighboring

Armenians in rejecting its teachings. But in 607 they broke with the Armenians and accepted it.

Monasticism began to flourish in Georgia in the 6th century, and reached its zenith in the 8th and 9th centuries. The monasteries became important centers of missionary and cultural activity. Georgians founded the Iviron monastery on Mount Athos, where many important religious works were translated from Greek into Georgian.

From the 11th to the 13th centuries, Georgia underwent a golden age during which a rich Christian literature was developed in the Georgian language. But this came to an end when the country was devastated by the invasions of Genghis Khan in the 13th century and Tamerlane in the 15th century. In the period 1500 to 1800 Georgia underwent a cultural renaissance, largely because the rival Ottomans and Persians kept each other from gaining full control over the country. New contacts were developed with the West and Russia.

In 1801 Georgia was annexed by Russia, and when the Patriarch died in 1811 the Russians abolished the Patriarchate. The Georgian Church was then administered from St. Petersburg by the Holy Synod of the Russian Orthodox Church through a special exarch. The 30 dioceses of the church were reduced to five, and the Georgian language was suppressed in the seminaries and in the liturgy, being replaced by Russian or Slavonic.

After the Bolshevik revolution of 1917, Georgia briefly regained its independence. The Georgian Church took this opportunity to declare that it was autocephalous once again, and to reestablish the Patriarchate, in 1918. This was accepted by the Moscow Patriarchate in 1943. On 4 March 1990, the Ecumenical Patriarchate confirmed both the autocephalous status of the Church of Georgia, and its patriarchal rank.

The situation of this church under Soviet rule was similar to that of the Russian Orthodox Church: while in 1917 there were 2,455 churches open in Georgia, only 80 were functioning by the mid-1980's. The Georgian Church was compelled to follow the Moscow Patriarchate in its ecumenical and international policies.

But the reform policies of Mikhail Gorbachev in the Soviet Union also affected the Church of Georgia. Many churches were re-opened, and on 1 October 1988 a Georgian Orthodox Theological Academy was formally inaugurated in Tbilisi, the capital, with 150 students studying in sections dealing with theology, Christian anthropology and Christian art.

The process of renewal intensified after Georgia became an independent nation in 1991. There were ample vocations to the priesthood, the beginnings of a renewal of monastic life, and many new churches were opened. The baptism of the Georgian President, Eduard Shevardnadze, into the Georgian Orthodox Church in late 1992 symbolized the augmented role that the church may be able to play in the newly-independent republic.

LOCATION: Georgia, small diaspora

HEAD: Catholicos Ilia II (born 1932, elected 1977)

Title: Catholicos-Patriarch of All Georgia

Residence: Tbilisi, Georgia

MEMBERSHIP: 3,000,000

## III. A. 10. The Orthodox Church of Cyprus

The Church of Cyprus traces its origins back to apostolic times, the island having been evangelized by Sts. Paul and Barnabas according to the Book of Acts (13:4-13). Because the island was administered as part of the civil province of the East, whose capital was Antioch, the Patriarchs of Antioch for a time claimed jurisdiction over the Cypriot Church and the right to appoint its Archbishop. But the Council of Ephesus in 431 recognized the church's independence and directed that the Archbishops of Cyprus should be elected by the synod of Cypriot bishops.

From the mid-7th century to the mid-10th century, there were frequent Arab attacks against Cyprus which often wrought widespread devastation. Because of this Arab threat, Byzantine Emperor Justinian II evacuated the Christian population of the island from 688 to 695, and settled many of them in a new city on the

Dardanelles called Nea Justiniana. The Archbishop of Cyprus took up residence there, and was given the additional title of Archbishop of Nea Justiniana, an honor which he retains to this day. The decisive victory of Byzantine Emperor Nicephorus II Phocas (963-969) over the Arabs inaugurated a period of peace during which churches and monasteries were rebuilt and the church flourished. In the 11th and 12th centuries, however, there was growing resentment against the oppressive rule of successive Byzantine governors who often used Cyprus as a basis for rebellion against the Emperors in Constantinople.

In 1191 the island was conquered by the English king Richard the Lionhearted, who had come to the area on a crusade. A few months later, Richard sold the island to the Knights Templar, who then sold it in 1192 to the Frenchman Guy de Lusignan, the exiled King of the Crusader state of Jerusalem. He established a western feudal society in Cyprus and a dynasty that would last nearly 300 years. A Latin hierarchy was soon erected, to the detriment of the Orthodox. By 1260 the Orthodox monasteries had been made subject to the Latin bishops, the number of Orthodox bishops on the island had been reduced from 15 to four, and all of them had been placed under the authority of the new Latin Archbishop of Cyprus. Several western monastic orders founded houses on the island, often benefiting from the confiscation of Orthodox ecclesiastical property. This situation changed little with the conquest of Cyprus by Venice in 1489.

In 1571 the island fell to the Ottoman Turks. The Turks ended the feudal social system, banished the Latin hierarchy, and recognized the Orthodox. Although the Orthodox were allowed to resume electing their own Archbishop, they retained only the four dioceses the Latins had allowed them. As was true elsewhere in the Ottoman Empire, the Orthodox bishops became civil as well as spiritual leaders of their own Greek people. Thus when the Greek revolution broke out in 1821, the bishops were considered sympathetic to the Greek cause. In the same year, all the bishops and many other prominent churchmen were summoned to the governor's palace and murdered by the guards. Later a new hierarchy was sent to the island by the Patriarchate of Antioch. These bishops were able to improve the situation of the Greek community somewhat, but it still suffered under very heavy taxation.

In 1878 Great Britain leased the island from Turkey and in 1914 annexed it outright. A political movement soon developed on Cyprus among the majority Greek community in favor of "enosis," or union with Greece. Orthodox religious leaders were involved in this movement, in keeping with their now traditional role in political affairs. When Britain granted independence to the island in 1960, the Archbishop of Cyprus, Makarios III, was elected its first president. Clashes between the Greek and Turkish communities culminated in 1974 with a Turkish invasion of the island and the establishment of a "Turkish Republic of Northern Cyprus." Many churches and monasteries in the northern part of the island were destroyed or looted in the process.

In April 1973 a crisis began in the Church of Cyprus when the three metropolitans of the island declared the deposition of Archbishop Makarios because his role as President was considered incompatible with being a bishop. But in July the three metropolitans were themselves deposed by a "major synod" made up of bishops from the Patriarchates of Alexandria, Antioch, Jerusalem, and the Church of Greece. New bishops were appointed, and the number of dioceses in Cyprus was later increased from four to six.

The Church of Cyprus administers Barnabas the Apostle Theological School in Nicosia. There are three men's and five women's monasteries directly dependent on the Archbishopric, and a number of smaller monasteries in the other dioceses.

LOCATION: Cyprus
HEAD: Archbishop Chrysostomos (born 1927, elected 1977)
Title: Archbishop of Nea Justiniana and All Cyprus
Residence: Nicosia, Cyprus
MEMBERSHIP: 442,000

## III. A. 11. The Orthodox Church of Greece

The Greek revolution against Turkish rule began in 1821 and culminated, after European intervention, in the recognition of the independence of a small Greek state by Turkey in 1832. The Orthodox Church played a prominent role in the revolution, and paid a heavy price for it: the Patriarch of Constantinople Gregorios V and a number of Metropolitans had been hanged by the Turks as traitors soon after the revolt broke out.

The new Greek government, in spite of traditional allegiances, was reluctant for the Orthodox Church in Greece to remain under the jurisdiction of the Patriarch of Constantinople, whose see remained in Ottoman territory. For this reason in 1833 the Church of Greece was declared autocephalous, and placed under the authority of a permanent five-member Synod of Bishops and the King, who was declared head of the church. The autocephalous status of the Greek Church was recognized in 1850 by Constantinople in a Patriarchal Tome which also specified that the Archbishop of Athens should be the permanent head of the synod of bishops.

As additional territory was incorporated into Greece at the expense of the Ottomans, new Orthodox dioceses were assimilated into the new Greek Church. The Orthodox in the extensive territory in northern Greece conquered from Turkey in 1912 remained directly under the jurisdiction of the Ecumenical Patriarchate until 1928 when by agreement it was "provisionally" placed under the administration of the Church of Greece.

State control over the Greek Church has been gradually reduced with the implementation of subsequent ecclesiastical regulations, although Orthodoxy was still recognized as the "dominant religion in Greece" in the latest constitution (1975). Today the supreme authority in the church is the synod of all functioning bishops. But most administrative matters are handled by a smaller permanent synod made up of 13 bishops including the Archbishop of Athens who presides over it.

Orthodox dioceses in Greece tend to be small: there were 81 in 1993. Monasticism has recently witnessed a modest revival, especially on Mount Athos, which remains the monastic center of the Orthodox world. Official statistics show that 96% of the population of Greece is Orthodox, 1% Catholic and Protestant, and 2% Muslim.

There was a significant renewal movement within the Greek Church following World War II. This was boosted by such movements as Zoe, the Orthodox Christian Unions, Apostoliki Diakonia, and Sotir. These groups, which often combine monastic spirituality with an active apostolate, resemble in some ways the apostolic religious communities which developed in the western church. The church has also been heavily involved in philanthropic activity, not only by issuing statements expressing the church's teaching on social justice, but also by maintaining many orphanages, homes for the aged, hospitals, etc.

Theological scholarship in Greece is centered at the two theological faculties at the universities of Athens and Thessalonika. There are also several seminaries for the training of parish priests. Many of the most distinguished theologians of the Greek Church are laymen.

The Greek Orthodox in the diaspora are under the jurisdiction of the Patriarchate of Constantinople [see III.A.1].

LOCATION: Greece
HEAD: Archbishop Seraphim (born 1913, elected 1974)
Title: Archbishop of Athens and All Greece
Residence: Athens, Greece
MEMBERSHIP: 9,025,000

## III. A. 12. The Orthodox Church of Poland

When Poland was restored as an independent country in the wake of World War I, nearly 4,000,000 Orthodox Christians were included within its new boundaries. Most of these were ethnic Belarusians and Ukrainians in the eastern parts of the country who had been under the jurisdiction of the Moscow Patriarchate.

Soon after its independence, however, the Polish government began to promote the idea that Orthodox in Poland should constitute an autocephalous Orthodox Church independent of Moscow. This position was supported by the first Orthodox Metropolitan of Warsaw, George Yoroshevsky, who had been recently appointed by Moscow and granted a certain degree of autonomy. But in 1923 he was assassinated by a Russian monk who held the opposite view.

The Polish government then appealed the question to the Patriarchate of Constantinople which, after lengthy consideration, issued a document granting autocephalous status to the Polish Orthodox Church on 13 November 1924. In 1927 Constantinople also granted the Metropolitan of Warsaw the title of "beatitude." The Moscow Patriarchate, however, considered this action as interference in its affairs, and refused to recognize the Polish Church's autocephalous status.

During the interwar period there was some tension within the Polish Orthodox Church deriving from the fact that all its bishops were Russian, while 70% of the faithful were Ukrainian. The bishops rejected demands for Ukrainian bishops and the use of the Ukrainian language in the liturgy, but took measures to satisfy many of these aspirations. During this period there were five dioceses, two seminaries (at Vilna and Krzemieniec) with 500 students, a Faculty of Orthodox Theology at Warsaw with 150 students, 1624 parishes, and 16 monasteries.

In the 1930's there were also some unfortunate conflicts between Catholics and Orthodox in Poland. Metropolitan Dionysy of Warsaw formally protested anti-Orthodox incidents, saying that Orthodox priests were being forced to preach in Polish, Orthodox churches were being forcibly closed and many destroyed, and that pressure was being placed on Orthodox faithful to become Catholic. The Ukrainian Catholic Metropolitan Andrew Sheptyckyj corroborated these accusations and added his own voice to the Orthodox protests in a pastoral letter to his faithful.

When Eastern Poland was annexed by the Soviet Union in 1939, most Polish Orthodox again found themselves in the Soviet Union and reincorporated into the Moscow Patriarchate. Thus the Polish Orthodox Church was greatly reduced in size.

In 1948, following the communist take-over of Poland, the Orthodox Metropolitan of Warsaw was deposed because of his opposition to communism. In the same year, at the request of the synod of Polish Orthodox bishops, the Moscow Patriarchate simultaneously declared Constantinople's 1924 proclamation of autocephaly null and void, and issued its own declaration of autocephaly. Nevertheless, the office of Metropolitan of Warsaw remained vacant until 1951 when the Polish Orthodox bishops asked the Moscow Patriarchate to name a new metropolitan. Moscow then appointed Archbishop Makary Oksaniuk of Lviv in Ukraine, who had presided over the dissolution of the Ukrainian Catholic Church in 1946-47, as new Metropolitan. Since that time, the Polish Orthodox Church has continued to have a close relationship with the Moscow Patriarchate.

In recent years, the Polish Orthodox Church has become more integrated into Polish culture, and Polish is being used in the liturgy more often. Four church periodicals are published, and the church is becoming increasingly involved in charitable works. The six dioceses and 250 parishes are served by about 300 priests. There are three small monasteries at Jableczna, Suprasl (near Bialystok), and Mount Grabarka. The Orthodox Theological Seminary in Warsaw has about 80 students, and there is an Orthodox faculty of theology at the Christian Theological Academy in the same city with 35 undergraduate students.

LOCATION: Poland
HEAD: Metropolitan Basil (born 1914, elected 1970)
Title: Metropolitan of Warsaw and All Poland
Residence: Warsaw, Poland
MEMBERSHIP: 1,000,000

## III. A. 13. The Orthodox Church of Albania

Christianity arrived in Albania before the 4th century from two directions. The Ghegs in the north of the country became Latin Christians, while the Byzantine tradition was predominant among the Tosk people in the south. But following the Turkish conquest in the 15th century, the majority of Albanians became Moslem. During

Turkish occupation, the remaining Orthodox population in Albania came under the jurisdiction of the Patriarchate of Constantinople.

Albania became an independent nation after the Balkan wars in 1912-1913, and almost immediately a movement for the independence of the Albanian Orthodox Church sprang up. After 1918 this movement was led by Fr. Fan Noli, an Albanian Orthodox priest from the United States. In 1922 an Orthodox Congress was held at Berat which unilaterally proclaimed the autocephalous status of the Albanian Orthodox Church. The Greek bishops then fled the country. In 1926 Constantinople offered an agreement which would have led to autocephaly, but the Albanian government rejected it. In 1929, Bishop John Bessarion, with the participation of a Serbian Orthodox bishop, ordained two additional Albanian Orthodox bishops. A synod of bishops was thus formed in Tirana and the church again declared itself autocephalous.

In reaction to this, Constantinople deposed the Albanian bishops, and the Albanian government in turn expelled the representative of Constantinople in the country. Thus a *de facto* schism was created. But Constantinople recognized the autocephalous status of the Albanian Orthodox Church and regularized the situation on 12 April 1937.

During the interwar period, aside from the Archbishopric of Tirana, there were Orthodox dioceses in Berat, Argyrokastro, and Korytsa. Greek was still widely used in the liturgy, but a process of translation of the texts into Albanian began in 1930. An Orthodox seminary was founded at Korytsa in 1937.

The communist revolution of 1945 marked the beginning of savage persecution of all religious groups in Albania. By this time the population was approximately 22% Orthodox and 10% Catholic. A number of influential Orthodox clergy were executed, and in 1949 Archbishop Christopher Kissi of Tirana was deposed. By 1951 all the Orthodox bishops had been replaced by men acceptable to the regime.

The Albanian government eventually took much stronger measures against religion than other governments in Eastern Europe. In 1967 it was announced that all religious edifices in Albania, including 2,169 churches, mosques, monasteries and other institutions had been closed, and all religious practices were declared illegal. In the same year, Orthodox Archbishop Damianos of Tirana was sent to prison where he died in 1973.

When the communist government in Albania began to disintegrate in 1990, the long period of religious persecution came to an end. Since no Albanian Orthodox bishops had survived, in January 1991 the Ecumenical Patriarchate, which had granted autocephalous status to the Albanian Church, appointed Metropolitan Anastasios of Androusis, a Professor at the University of Athens, as Patriarchal Exarch in Albania. It was his task to oversee the process of the canonical reconstruction of the autocephalous Albanian Orthodox Church. On 24 June 1992, the Holy Synod of the Ecumenical Patriarchate elected Anastasios as Archbishop of Tirana and All Albania, and named three other bishops for the remaining Orthodox dioceses in the country. Anastasios was enthroned the following August, but by mid-1993 the government had not yet confirmed the other three bishops. Thus the Albanian Orthodox Church, whose hierarchy had been destroyed by the communist regime, was reconstituted.

By early 1993, the Albanian Orthodox Church had regained 25 of the 324 churches that had been confiscated by the communist regime. A theological seminary has been opened in an abandoned hotel in Durrës, where about 80 young men are studying for the priesthood. Already 28 priests and nine deacons have been ordained.

In North America there are two separate Albanian Orthodox jurisdictions. The Albanian Orthodox Archdiocese in America, which makes up a distinct ethnic diocese within the Orthodox Church in America [see III.A.15] and has 13 parishes, is currently administered by Metropolitan Theodosius. The diocesan chancery is at 519 East Broadway, South Boston, Massachusetts 02127.

In addition, the Albanian Orthodox Diocese in America, which has two parishes, is under the spiritual care of the Greek Orthodox Archdiocese of North and South America [see III.C.4].

LOCATION: Albania, small diaspora

HEAD: Metropolitan Anastasios (born 1929, elected 1992)

Title: Archbishop of Tirana and All Albania
Residence: Tirana, Albania
MEMBERSHIP: 160,000

## III. A. 14. The Orthodox Church in the Czech and Slovak Republics

At the time of its founding as an independent state after World War I, Czechoslovakia was a preponderantly Catholic nation. But soon after independence, a number of Catholic priests and faithful decided to become Orthodox. The elected leader of the movement, Fr. Matej Pavlik, was ordained a bishop in 1921 by a Serbian Orthodox bishop in Belgrade, and assumed the name Gorazd. But the larger part of this group soon split away and formed a Protestant Church. At this point the Orthodox group numbered about 40,000. Their number soon increased when some Byzantine Catholics in Transcarpathia became Orthodox.

Subsequent developments led to divisions within the Orthodox community in the country. In 1923 the Patriarchate of Constantinople granted the Czechoslovak Church autonomous status and sent Metropolitan Sabbazd to look after the Orthodox faithful there. And in 1930 the Serbian Patriarchate sent a bishop of its own to Transcarpathia. Most Orthodox Czechoslovaks, however, remained within Bishop Gorazd's jurisdiction.

During World War II, this church was virtually annihilated by the Nazis, who executed Bishop Gorazd and his close associates in 1942. All the priests were sent to German labor camps.

In the 1931 census, there were 145,583 Orthodox in the country, 117,897 of them being in Transcarpathia. The annexation of that region by the Soviet Union in 1945 reduced the number of Orthodox in Czechoslovakia to about 40,000. In 1946 the Czechoslovak Orthodox placed themselves under the protection of the Russian Patriarch Alexis, and asked him to send them a bishop. All the Orthodox in the country were now united under a single hierarchy.

In 1950 the Byzantine Catholics in Slovakia were absorbed into the Czechoslovak Orthodox Church [see Slovak Catholic Church: IV.D.8]. This brought about 200,000 new members into the church which in the same year was reorganized into four dioceses. But most of these new members were lost again when the Byzantine Catholic Church in Slovakia was allowed to resume functioning during the "Prague Spring" of 1968. Church buildings, however, were left in the hands of the Orthodox.

On 9 December 1951, the Patriarchate of Moscow granted autocephalous status to the Orthodox Church of Czechoslovakia, but this has not been recognized by the Patriarchate of Constantinople.

In its first act of the kind, the Czechoslovak Church canonized Bishop Gorazd in September 1987 because of the central role he played in the formation of the Orthodox Church in that country, and his martyrdom for the faith.

The collapse of the communist government in 1989, and the subsequent division of Czechoslovakia into independent Czech and Slovak states on 1 January 1993, required modifications in the structure of this Orthodox Church. In November 1992 the Holy Synod decided to divide into two metropolitan provinces, with two dioceses in each of the new republics. In this arrangement, Metropolitan Nicholas of Prešov is head of the Orthodox Church in Slovakia. But the united Holy Synod will continue to meet periodically as before, under the presidency of Metropolitan Dorotheos of Prague.

In Slovakia the government has decided to return most Greek Catholic churches that were confiscated in 1950 to their earlier owners. As a result, it was reported in March 1993 that 135 of the 170 Orthodox churches in Slovakia had been taken given to the Greek Catholics. Candidates for the Orthodox priesthood are educated at the Orthodox Theological Faculty at Prešov.

LOCATION: The Czech Republic and Slovakia

HEAD: Metropolitan Dorotheos (born 1913, elected 1964)

Title: Metropolitan of Prague and Archbishop of the Czech and
    Slovak Republics
Residence: Prague, Czech Republic
MEMBERSHIP: 55,000


## III. A. 15. The Orthodox Church in America

Orthodoxy arrived in North America when a band of Russian
Orthodox missionaries from Valaam monastery reached Alaska in
1794. At that time, Alaska was a Russian imperial province. A first
church was built on Kodiak Island, and a number of Eskimos and
Indians were baptized. In 1840 a diocese was erected for Kamchatka,
the Kurile and Aleutian Islands, with its see at Sitka. The first bishop
was Innocent Veniaminov, who was later to become the
Metropolitan of Moscow. By 1868, when Alaska was sold to the
United States, the Russian mission was flourishing among the
Eskimos, and had translated the Bible and the Orthodox liturgy into
the native Aleut language.

The headquarters of the diocese was transferred from Sitka to San
Francisco in 1872. In 1890 an auxiliary bishop was given pastoral
responsibilities in Alaska, and in 1906 Sitka again became the seat of
a separate Russian Orthodox diocese of Alaska. In 1905 Bishop
Tikhon (later the ill-fated Patriarch of Moscow) had moved his see
from San Francisco to New York. In 1907 he was granted the title
Archbishop, with suffragans in Brooklyn and Alaska.

A significant number of Byzantine Catholics joined the Russian
Orthodox Church in America in the late 19th century. This was the
result of the disapproval of the presence of married Byzantine
Catholic priests in their dioceses by some Roman Catholic bishops.
Archbishop John Ireland of St. Paul, for instance, refused to accept
Fr. Alexis Tóth (1854-1909) as pastor of the Ruthenian Catholic parish
in Minneapolis because he was a widower. As a result, Tóth and his
parishioners entered into the Russian Orthodox Church in 1891. Tóth
eventually founded 17 Orthodox parishes in the USA for erstwhile
Ruthenian Catholics.

Following the Bolshevik Revolution in Russia in 1917, there was a large influx of Russian immigrants into America. Many of these Russian Orthodox were critical of their mother Church because of its policy of cooperation with the Soviet authorities. For this reason, in April 1924 the North American Diocese declared itself a temporarily self-governing church while retaining spiritual communion with the Church of Russia.

In 1935, an agreement was reached with the Russian Orthodox Church Outside Russia [see III.D.2], which had broken with the Moscow Patriarchate, according to which the North American "Metropolia" would be considered one of its districts, but would remain independent in practice.

But by 1946 it had become clear that the Russian Orthodox Church Outside Russia lacked canonical legitimacy in the eyes of most Orthodox Churches. Therefore, the Metropolia decided to again recognize the Patriarch of Moscow as its spiritual head on the condition that their church retain complete administrative autonomy.

In 1970, the Moscow Patriarchate granted autocephalous status to the Metropolia, calling it the Orthodox Church in America (also known simply as "the OCA"). Those parishes which wished to remain directly under Moscow's supervision were allowed to do so [see III.A.5]. This action provoked an exchange of letters between Moscow and Constantinople in which the Ecumenical Patriarchate challenged Moscow's authority to grant autocephalous status to its daughter church. The autocephaly of the OCA was subsequently recognized, however, by the Orthodox Churches of Bulgaria, Georgia, Poland, and Czechoslovakia.

This dispute has still not been resolved. However, there have been significant contacts between the OCA and the Ecumenical Patriarchate. OCA delegations visited Istanbul in 1990 and 1991, and another encounter took place during Patriarch Dimitrios' visit to the United States in July 1991. Metropolitan Theodosius himself led a delegation to the Patriarchate in December 1992. They were received by Patriarch Bartholomew and had meetings with the Synodical

Commission for Inter-Orthodox Affairs. Both sides expressed a commitment to Orthodox canonical unity and order in America.

In practice, the OCA is in communion with the rest of the Orthodox Churches, and its bishops take part in the Standing Conference of Canonical Orthodox Bishops in America. But the OCA has not been able to participate in pan-Orthodox activities such as the international theological dialogues with other Christian communions because it lacks the necessary unanimous recognition of its status as autocephalous or autonomous by the other Orthodox Churches.

Three other Orthodox jurisdictions of different ethnic backgrounds have come into full canonical union with the OCA, giving it a multi-ethnic character. These are an Albanian Diocese with 13 parishes, a Bulgarian Diocese with 16 parishes, and a Romanian Diocese with 59 parishes.

There are 15 monastic communities under the direct jurisdiction of the Primate. The largest of these are New Skete Monastery (11 monks) and the affiliated Monastery of Our Lady of the Sign (10 nuns) in Cambridge, New York, and St. Tikhon's Monastery (12 monks) in South Canaan, Pennsylvania. The Romanian Diocese has Holy Transfiguration Monastery in Elwood City, Pennsylvania (11 nuns).

At present there are three theological schools administered by the OCA. St. Herman's Orthodox Theological Seminary in Kodiak, Alaska, was founded in 1973 for the training of Alaska Native clergy and church workers. St. Tikhon's Seminary at South Canaan, Pennsylvania, was founded in 1937 and is affiliated with St. Tikhon's Monastery. But the largest and most important school is St. Vladimir's Orthodox Theological Seminary in Crestwood, New York.

In the United States, there is a total of 13 dioceses and 470 parishes. The ethnic dioceses extend into Canada, which also has one non-ethnic diocese presided over by Bishop Seraphim (elected October 1990). Altogether there are 76 Canadian parishes. The OCA has a Mexican Exarchate with 13 parishes, and 9 parishes in South America. In addition, there are three parishes in Australia under the

OCA's canonical protection. Contact Fr. T. Michaluk at the Russian American Orthodox Church of St. Michael, 38 Wentworth Road, PO Box 106, Homebush NSW 2140.

LOCATION: North America

HEAD: Metropolitan Theodosius (born 1933, elected 1977)

Title: Archbishop of Washington, Metropolitan of All America and Canada

Address: P.O. Box 675
 Syosset, New York 11791

MEMBERSHIP: 1,000,000

## III. B. The Autonomous Orthodox Churches

There are four Orthodox Churches which, although functioning as independent Churches on a day-to-day basis, have a certain dependency on another Orthodox Church. In practice this usually means that the head of an autonomous church must be confirmed in his office by the head or synod of an autocephalous Church. The Orthodox Church of Finland is dependent on the Ecumenical Patriarchate, and Mount Sinai is dependent on the Patriarchate of Jerusalem. The Moscow Patriarchate has granted autonomous status to its Orthodox daughter Churches in Japan and China, but this has not been recognized by Constantinople.

## III. B. 1. The Orthodox Church of Mount Sinai

Given its importance as the site where, according to the Book of Exodus, Moses received the Books of the Law from God, Mount Sinai has been frequented by Christian pilgrims since ancient times. By the third century, Christian anchorites had begun to live in the area, and by the fourth century they had formed one or more communities of monks.

Because the area had become unstable and the monks vulnerable to attack, the Emperor Justinian decided to fortify the monastery in 528. He also settled 200 families from Egypt and Trebizond in the area to protect and serve the monastic community.

At first the monastery had a highly international character, with Slavic, Arab, Latin, Armenian, Ethiopian and Syrian monks, as well as Greeks. Perhaps the best known monk of the monastery was St. John Climacus, who was Abbot in the 7th century. By that time, the area had been conquered by the Moslem Arabs. Islamic governments were generally tolerant towards the monastery, but on several occasions wild tribes in the area ravaged the monastery, requiring the monks to temporarily close it and take refuge in Cairo or

Alexandria. During this period, monks of other nationalities abandoned the monastery to the Greeks.

St. Catherine's monastery, as it has been known since the 9th century, was originally part of the Patriarchate of Jerusalem, within the diocese of Pharan. After the bishop of Pharan was deposed for monotheletism in 681, the see was transferred to the monastery itself, the abbot becoming the bishop of Pharan. With the subsequent union of the diocese of Raitho with the monastery, all the Christians in the Sinai peninsula came under the jurisdiction of the abbot-archbishop.

In 1575 the Patriarchate of Constantinople granted Mount Sinai autonomous status. This was reaffirmed in 1782. The only remaining link with the Jerusalem Patriarchate is that the abbot, who is elected by an assembly of senior monks, must be ordained a bishop by the Jerusalem Patriarch, who is also commemorated in the monastery's liturgy.

The monastery's library is world-famous for its great antiquity and its manuscripts. It was here in 1859 that Tischendorf found the "Codex Sinaiticus" of the Bible. Today it contains about 4,000 manuscripts. Some of the world's most ancient icons are also found in the monastery, which was already outside the Byzantine Empire during the iconoclast controversy when most icons in the Empire were destroyed.

Currently the monastery, aside from the library, has a guest house and a hospital for the local population. The monks also administer a school in Cairo. The monastery has historically had many dependent churches and monasteries ("metochia") in other countries. At present there are one in Cairo (where the Abbot often resides), seven in Greece, three in Cyprus, one in Lebanon and one in Istanbul, Turkey.

Today, aside from the 20 or so monks in the monastic community, this Church includes a few hundred Bedouins and fishermen who live in the Sinai. There was an agreement between the Greek and Egyptian governments in 1984 which allowed for up to 50 new Greek monks to be received by the monastery.

Beginning in the period following the Israeli invasion in 1967, perhaps the greatest problem facing the community has been maintaining an authentic monastic lifestyle while dealing with a massive influx of tourists. This problem has continued after the area's return to Egyptian administration.

LOCATION: Sinai peninsula, Egypt.

HEAD: Archbishop Damianos (born 1935, elected 1973)

Title: Abbot of St. Catherine's Monastery, Archbishop of Sinai, Pharan, and Raitho.

Residence: Cairo, Egypt

MEMBERSHIP: 900


## III. B. 2. The Orthodox Church of Finland

Although it appears that the earliest Finnish Christians were Byzantines, most of the country received the Christian faith in its Latin form through the activity of Swedish missionaries. The easternmost Finnish province of Karelia, however, was evangelized by Byzantine monks from the ancient monastery of Valamo ("Valaam" in Russian) located on an island in Lake Ladoga.

In the 13th century Finland was a battleground between Catholic Sweden and Orthodox Russia. Eventually Sweden gained control of most of Finland, but Karelia came under Russian control.

But in 1617 Karelia was also taken over by Sweden, which had in the meantime adopted the Lutheran faith. This began a period of persecution of the Orthodox which subsided, however, in the later part of the century.

Karelia was again occupied by Russia in 1721, and in 1809 the Czar conquered all of Finland, which then became an autonomous Grand Duchy within the Russian Empire. Later in the 19th century Orthodox Karelians began to assert their national identity. The liturgy and many Orthodox theological and spiritual works were translated into Finnish, which remains the liturgical language of this church.

In 1917 Finland gained its independence from Russia, and in 1918 the Orthodox in Finland declared themselves an autonomous church in relation to Moscow. Patriarch Tikhon of Moscow recognized this status in 1921. But in 1923, the Finnish Orthodox Church was placed under the protection of the Patriarchate of Constantinople.

The 1939-40 Winter War between Finland and the Soviet Union resulted in the loss of 90% of the property belonging to the Finnish Orthodox Church when most of Karelia was annexed by the USSR. Most Orthodox Finns were evacuated to other parts of Finland and began new lives scattered across the country.

In 1957 the Moscow Patriarchate recognized the Finnish Orthodox Church's autonomy under the Ecumenical Patriarchate. In 1980 the General Assembly of the Finnish Orthodox Church voted to seek autocephalous status from the Ecumenical Patriarchate, but no action has yet been taken on this proposal.

There is a long history of monasticism in the Finnish Orthodox Church. But the monasteries had to be evacuated as a result of the Russo-Finnish War because they were now located in Soviet-occupied territory. The famous Valamo Monastery was refounded at Heinvesi in central Finland, and became known as New Valamo. The community also included monks from other Karelian monasteries. Lintula Convent was also refounded near New Valamo. Today these two monasteries are important centers of Finnish Orthodox spiritual life.

A Finnish Orthodox Seminary had been founded at Sortavala in Karelia in 1918, just after Finland became independent. But after the city was annexed by the Soviets in 1940, the seminary had to be moved to Helsinki. It was transferred to Humaljrvi in 1957, and to Kuopio four years later. It was officially closed on 31 July 1988 in order to make way for the establishment of a Department of Orthodox Theology at the University of Joensuu, which began functioning in the fall of 1988.

When a new Archbishop of Finland is chosen, his election must be confirmed by the Ecumenical Patriarchate. Even though theirs is not an autocephalous church, Finnish Orthodox representatives now take part in all pan-Orthodox activities alongside delegates of the autocephalous Orthodox Churches.

The government of Finland recognizes the Finnish Orthodox Church as the second national church, after the predominant

Evangelical-Lutheran Church. This is the only Orthodox Church which follows the western dates for Easter and fixed feasts.

LOCATION: Finland
HEAD: Archbishop John (born 1923, elected 1987)
Title: Archbishop of Karelia and All Finland
Residence: Kuopio, Finland
MEMBERSHIP: 52,500


## III. B. 3. The Orthodox Church of Japan

This church began in 1861 with the arrival in Japan of a young Russian missionary priest-monk named Nicholas Kassathin. Before his death in 1912, he had baptized some 20,000 Japanese into the Orthodox faith and had translated the New Testament and many liturgical books into Japanese. Because of his central role in the foundation of the Orthodox Church in Japan, he was canonized in 1970.

Orthodoxy in Japan quickly became an indigenous phenomenon, which enabled it to survive periods of hostility between Japan and Russia. This process was completed with the installation of Bishop Theodosius as the first native Japanese Metropolitan in 1972.

As a result of canonical problems with the Russian Orthodox Church in the period following the Bolshevik Revolution, the Orthodox Church in Japan placed itself under the jurisdiction of the American Metropolia [see the OCA: III.A.15] from 1945 to 1970. When the Orthodox Church in America was declared autocephalous by the Moscow Patriarchate in 1970, the OCA returned the Japanese Orthodox Church to the jurisdiction of Moscow, and Moscow simultaneously declared the Japanese Church autonomous. Consequently, the election of the head of the Japanese Orthodox Church must now be confirmed by the Moscow Patriarchate. The autonomy of the Japanese Church has not been recognized, however, by the Ecumenical Patriarchate and most other Orthodox Churches.

At present there are three dioceses with about 30 priests serving approximately 100 worshiping communities. All the clergy are now of Japanese origin, and are trained at a seminary in Tokyo.

LOCATION: Japan
HEAD: Metropolitan Theodosius (born 1935, elected 1972)
Title: Archbishop of Tokyo, Metropolitan of All Japan
Residence: Tokyo, Japan
MEMBERSHIP: 25,000

## III. B. 4. The Orthodox Church of China

The origins of Chinese Orthodoxy can be traced back to 1686, when the Chinese Emperor hired a group of Russian Cossacks as his personal bodyguard. Their descendants were eventually completely absorbed into Chinese culture, but remained Orthodox in faith and formed the nucleus of an Orthodox community in China.

The Russian Orthodox Church began missionary activity in China at the end of the 19th century. By 1914 there were about 5,000 Chinese Orthodox, including Chinese priests and a seminary in Peking.

After the 1917 Russian revolution, Russian emigrés swelled the Orthodox population in China. In 1939 there were 5 bishops in the country and an Orthodox University at Harbin. By 1949 there were 100,000 faithful, 60 parishes, 200 priests, 2 monasteries and a seminary in Manchuria, as well as 150 parishes and 200,000 faithful in the rest of China.

After the communist revolution in China, most of the Russian clergy and faithful were either repatriated to the Soviet Union or fled to the West. By 1955, there were only 30 Russian priests left.

The Moscow Patriarchate granted autonomous status to the Chinese Orthodox Church in 1957, and recalled its Russian hierarchy. At that time there were about 20,000 faithful with two bishops in Shanghai and Peking. Little is known about the present situation of this church.

Location: China
MEMBERSHIP: 20,000 (?)


## III. C. Canonical Churches Under Constantinople

These are churches which, often because of political turmoil in their countries of origin, have been received under the canonical protection of the Ecumenical Patriarchate. Thus they are considered entirely legitimate, but particular arrangements have had to be made for them in their special circumstances. The Ecumenical Patriarchate provides these churches with the Holy Chrism, and names their bishops.


### III. C. 1. The American Carpatho-Russian Orthodox Greek Catholic Diocese of the U.S.A

This church exists only in the United States, and is made up of descendants of Ruthenian Catholic [see Ruthenian Catholic Church, IV.D.3] immigrants from a section of the Austro-Hungarian Empire known as Subcarpathia or Transcarpathia, now in western Ukraine just east of the Slovak and Hungarian borders.

When they immigrated to the United States in the 19th century, these Ruthenian Catholics were often accompanied by their own married priests. The presence of married Catholic priests within their dioceses often evoked the disapproval of local Roman Catholic bishops.

In 1929 a Vatican Decree, *Cum Data Fuerit*, was issued. It stated that newly ordained and newly arrived Eastern rite priests in North America were henceforth to be celibate in spite of the terms of union with Rome which had guaranteed Ruthenian Catholics the right to retain married clergy. This gave rise to widespread dismay in the Eastern rite Catholic community.

In 1937 a meeting was held in Pittsburgh, Pennsylvania, of disaffected Ruthenian Catholics under the leadership of Fr. Orestes Chornock. The assembly decided to petition the Patriarchate of Constantinople to received the group into the Orthodox Church, and to ordain Fr. Chornock as its first bishop, consolidating them into a distinct diocese. Constantinople approved the request, and Fr. Chornock was ordained to the episcopate at the Ecumenical Patriarchate in 1938. The new diocese was placed under the spiritual supervision of the Greek Orthodox Archdiocese of North and South America.

A seminary was founded in New York City soon after the establishment of the diocese. After several transfers, in 1951 it was permanently moved to Johnstown, Pennsylvania, and named Christ the Savior Seminary.

LOCATION: The United States

HEAD: Bishop Nicholas of Amissos (born 1936, elected 1985)

Residence: 312 Garfield Street

Johnstown, Pennsylvania 15906

MEMBERSHIP: 75 parishes and 4 missions, 100,000 members

## III. C. 2. Ukrainian Orthodox Church in America

This jurisdiction was formed in response to the concerns of some Orthodox Ukrainians who wanted to establish communion with the canonical Orthodox Church. Many of them were members of the Ukrainian Autocephalous Orthodox Church [see III.D.3].

In the mid-1930's, a group of these Ukrainians petitioned Archbishop Athenagoras (Greek Orthodox Primate of North and South America) to provide them with a canonical Ukrainian bishop who would be under the jurisdiction of the Ecumenical Patriarchate. They were led by a former Greek Catholic priest, Fr. Bogdan Spilka. This request was approved by the Holy Synod of the Patriarchate of Constantinople on 28 February 1937, and Fr. Bogdan was subsequently ordained the group's first bishop.

There followed a period of competition between the two Ukrainian jurisdictions, with a number of parishes shifting from one side to the other. After the death of Bishop Bogdan in 1965, an effort was made to reconcile the two groups, but to no avail.

Unlike the Ukrainian Orthodox Church, this diocese uses traditional Church Slavonic in the liturgy instead of Ukrainian. It remains under the spiritual supervision of the Greek Orthodox Archdiocese of North and South America. At present there are 20 parishes in the United States and 8 in Canada.

LOCATION: The United States and Canada
HEAD: Bishop Vsevolod of Scopelos (born 1927, elected 1987)
Residence: 90-34 139th Street
Jamaica, New York, 11435 USA
MEMBERSHIP: 50,000

## III. C. 3. The Russian Orthodox Archdiocese in Western Europe

After the Bolshevik Revolution in Russia in 1917, many Russian Orthodox faithful and clergy found themselves in exile outside the Soviet Union. A group of Russian Orthodox bishops met in Constantinople in 1920 to form an autonomous church which would reestablish relations with the Moscow Patriarchate as soon as conditions allowed. This provided the nucleus of what would become the Russian Orthodox Church Outside Russia [see III.D.2].

This Synod of bishops, which took a strongly anti-communist political position, was condemned by Patriarch Tikhon, who in 1921 appointed Metropolitan Evlogius as his legitimate representative in Western Europe, based in Paris. In 1927 the Synod "suspended" Metropolitan Evlogius and broke communion with him. This effectively split the Russian emigré community in Europe between those loyal to the Synod in exile and those loyal to the Patriarchate through Evlogius.

In 1928 Metropolitan Sergei (then patriarchal *locum tenens*) called on all Russian bishops to refrain from political activity and to recognize the Soviet regime. Evlogius initially accepted this, but in 1930 he took part in an Anglican prayer service in London for persecuted Christians in the Soviet Union. In response, Metropolitan Sergei removed Evlogius from office and appointed another bishop for Patriarchal parishes in Western Europe.

Most Russian Orthodox bishops and faithful of this jurisdiction remained loyal to Evlogius, however, and considered Metropolitan Sergei's call for acceptance of the Soviet regime unacceptable. Evlogius then petitioned the Ecumenical Patriarchate's assistance, and in 1931 Patriarch Photius II received Evlogius and his followers under the jurisdiction of Constantinople.

The best-known institution belonging to this archdiocese is St. Sergius Orthodox Theological Institute in Paris. It was founded by Metropolitan Evlogius in 1925, and is recognized world-wide as an intellectual center of Orthodox theology.

LOCATION: Western Europe
HEAD: Archbishop Sergei Konovalov (elected 1993)
Title: Russian Orthodox Archbishop of Western Europe
Residence: Paris, France
MEMBERSHIP: about 100,000

## III. C. 4. The Albanian Orthodox Diocese of America

After the establishment of a communist government in Albania after World War II and the destruction of the Albanian Orthodox Church [see III.A.13] in 1967, Albanian Orthodox in the diaspora, located mainly in the United States, found themselves without a mother church. The majority eventually formed the Albanian Orthodox Archdiocese in America, which joined the Orthodox Church in America [see III.A.15].

But a small group preferred to come directly under the jurisdiction of the Patriarchate of Constantinople, and formed this Albanian Orthodox Diocese of America. At present, its two parishes are headed by a vicar priest who is directly responsible to Archbishop Iakovos of the Greek Orthodox Archdiocese of North and South America.

LOCATION: The United States
HEAD: Rev. Ilia Katre, Vicar General
Residence: 6455 Silver Dawn Lane, Las Vegas, Nevada 89118
MEMBERSHIP: 5,100

## III. C. 5. The Belarusian Council of Orthodox Churches in North America

This is a group of four Belarusian Orthodox [see III.D.4] parishes in the United States and one in Canada which have placed themselves under the jurisdiction of the Ecumenical Patriarchate. They do not have a bishop of their own, but are under the care of an administrator. He is directly responsible to Archbishop Iakovos of the Greek Orthodox Archdiocese of North and South America.

LOCATION: The United States and Canada
HEAD: Very Rev. Sviatoslaw Kous, Administrator
Residence: P.O. Box 26, South River, New Jersey 08882, USA

## III. C. 6. The Ukrainian Orthodox Church of Canada

In 1918 a group of Ukrainian Greek Catholics in Canada, fearing that as Catholics their Ukrainian identity could not be preserved, decided to become Orthodox. The situation of Orthodox in Canada being confused by the effects of the Bolshevik revolution in Russia, it was some time before the group found a permanent jurisdiction to which it could belong. But in late 1919, the group was received into communion with the self-proclaimed Ukrainian Autocephalous Orthodox Church [see III.D.3 below]. Archbishop John Teodorovich, who had been ordained uncanonically in Ukraine, became the first head of the new church. Archbishop John later tried to regularize the status of his church and seek reconsecration by the Ecumenical Patriarch in Constantinople, but his church council did not allow him to proceed.

This original group of former Byzantine Catholics was strengthened when Orthodox from Ukraine later began to arrive in Canada in large numbers. It was to become the largest Orthodox community in Canada, having some 50 parishes by 1940.

In 1945 Archbishop John resigned and the church council voted to break off relations with the Ukrainian Autocephalous Church in Ukraine which had been suppressed by the Soviet government. Relations were established with the Ukrainian Autocephalous Church Abroad, then based in western Europe. In the same year, St. Andrew's Institute was set up in Winnipeg to provide theological education for the clergy.

By 1955 the Ukrainian Orthodox Church in Canada had 270 parishes and 76 priests. In 1960 St. Andrew's Institute was moved to a new location and affiliated with the University of Manitoba. The church now had some 140,000 members.

New efforts to regularize this church's canonical status began in the late 1980's, and culminated in the official reception of the Ukrainian Greek Orthodox Church of Canada into the jurisdiction of the Ecumenical Patriarchate of Constantinople on 1 April 1990. There are bishops in Winnipeg, Saskatoon and Edmonton.

Although there have been some attempts to use English in the liturgy this has been repeatedly condemned by the church consistory. St. Andrew's Institute remains the only Orthodox theological school in the country.

LOCATION: Canada
HEAD: Metropolitan Wasyly (born 1909, elected 1985)
Title: Metropolitan of Winnipeg and All Canada
Residence: 174 Seven Oaks, Winnipeg, Manitoba R2V 0K8
MEMBERSHIP: 200,000

## III. D. Orthodox Churches of Irregular Status

The canonical status of all the churches in this group is questioned in some way by Orthodoxy as a whole. This is not to put them all on the same level, as some are considered simply uncanonical, while others are in full schism and out of communion with the Orthodox Church.

## III. D. 1. The Old Believers

The "Old Believers" came into existence as the result of a schism within the Russian Orthodox Church in the 17th century. The Russian Church had adopted certain liturgical usages which differed from those of the Greeks. Patriarch Nikon (1605-1681) introduced changes intended to "correct" these Russian practices and make them conform to Greek usage. This was offensive to some Russian Orthodox who affirmed that it was legitimate for the Russian Church to adopt its own traditions. Opposition coalesced around a priest named Avvakum, who was burnt at the stake in 1682. His followers became known as Old Believers, or those who followed the old rituals which predated the reform.

The Old Believers were harshly persecuted under the czars. Many fled into Asia in the 18th century and others were forcefully exiled from European Russia. Many communities lived in almost complete isolation for centuries. Since no Orthodox bishop had joined the Old Believers, the group was deprived of a hierarchy. This, along with the fact that the communities were spread over vast areas, caused them to split into as many as 12 groups, each with its own characteristics.

The two most important groups are known as "Popovtsy," who have retained priests and sacraments, and "Bezpopovtsy," who reject them. The priestless communities are scattered throughout the far north from Karelia to the Urals. In 1847 the former Greek Orthodox bishop Ambrosios of Sarajevo (Bosnia) embraced the Old Believers and consecrated two bishops for those who remained loyal to the priesthood and sacraments. This gave rise to the hierarchy of the largest priestly group.

It was only in 1905, with the issuing of an Edict of Tolerance by the Czar, that Old Believers were granted a status equal to that of other religions in Russia. The situation of this community since the

Bolshevik Revolution of 1917 is poorly known, but there have been attempts to overcome the schism. Metropolitan Sergei and the Holy Synod took unsuccessful measures to heal the rift in 1929. Meetings took place in the period following World War II which culminated in the solemn lifting of the anathemas in 1971. So far this act has not, however, resulted in reestablishment of communion between Old Believers and the Russian Orthodox Church.

The Old Believers are legally recognized in Russia, but are believed to have substantially declined in numbers since the Soviet revolution. There are five Old Believer parishes in the United States, and about 500 members in Canada. In Australia contact Mr. Moisey Ovchinnikoff at the Old Orthodox Church of Holy Nativity, 20 Norval Street, Auburn NSW 2144.

LOCATION: Russia, diaspora
MEMBERSHIP: 2,500,000?

## III. D. 2. The Russian Orthodox Church Outside Russia

Following the Bolshevik Revolution of 1917, over a million Russians found themselves in exile scattered in many countries. Many of these had fled the country after the defeat of the white armies which had attempted to destroy the new Soviet regime, and a significant number of clergy came with them.

In 1920 there was a meeting of over 20 Russian Orthodox bishops in Constantinople. They decided to create temporarily an autonomous church for the emigré Russians, intending to reestablish canonical links with the Moscow Patriarchate when conditions permitted. A synod of bishops was established under the presidency of Anthony Khrapovitsky, the exiled Metropolitan of Kiev. At the invitation of the Serbian Orthodox Church, they established their headquarters at Karlovci, Yugoslavia.

The monarchist political views of this group became clear when in 1921 the Synod formally called for the restoration of the Romanov dynasty in Russia. Patriarch Tikhon denounced the Synod for this in May 1922. The Synod broke with Metropolitan Evlogius of Paris in

1927 [see the Russian Orthodox Archdiocese of Western Europe: III.C.3]. In 1928, after the Karlovci synod flatly refused to accept the call of Metropolitan Sergei (Patriarchal *locum tenens*) for all Russian bishops to refrain from political activity, Sergei ordered that the synod be dissolved. In 1934 Sergei and the Russian Orthodox Synod in Moscow formally suspended all the bishops of the Karlovci synod pending an ecclesiastical trial which, in fact, has never taken place.

Most of the bishops of the Synod either did not survive World War II, or were reconciled individually to the Moscow Patriarchate. But the group was reinforced after the war by Orthodox bishops who had ministered in the Nazi-occupied regions of the Soviet Union, and who subsequently fled the country. The headquarters of the Synod had been moved from Karlovci to Munich during the war, and in 1950 it was moved to the United States.

There have been a number of appeals from the Moscow Patriarchate for this group to return to canonical communion with it, but so far to no avail. In 1974 Patriarch Pimen sent a message to the Synod's Sobor of Bishops, Clergy, and Laity, in which he invited them only to recognize the validity of the Moscow Patriarchate and allow intercommunion with it. Moscow no longer requested that they also support the Soviet State. To the present, however, the Synod continues to deny the ecclesial nature of the Moscow Patriarchate, as well as such churches as the Orthodox Church in America who are in full communion with it. The local council of the Russian Orthodox Church that was held in Zagorsk in June 1988 on the occasion of the millennium of the Baptism of Rus issued an appeal for the canonical unity of all Russian Orthodox, and expressed the hope that a dialogue for this purpose might soon begin.

After the fall of the communist government and the dissolution of the Soviet Union, the Russian Orthodox Church Outside Russia began to establish itself in Russia. By January 1992 it claimed to have just over 50 worshiping communities in the country under the pastoral guidance of three bishops.

The Synod remains very conservative in character, and strongly opposed to the modern ecumenical movement. Its monarchist political views came to the fore recently when it canonized Czar Nicholas II and his family.

At present there are some 109 worshiping communities of the Russian Orthodox Church Outside Russia in the United States, and 19 in Canada. There are several monasteries, the most important of which is Holy Trinity Monastery in Jordanville, New York, which has 24 monks. There are ten communities in the United Kingdom under the spiritual guidance of Bishop Mark (14 St. Dunstan's Road, Barons Court, London W6). Bishop Daniel is currently *locum tenens* for the 20 parishes in Australia and 2 in New Zealand (PO Box 38, 20 Chelmsford Avenue, Croydon, NSW 2132).

LOCATION: Worldwide and recently again in Russia

HEAD: Metropolitan Vitaly (born 1910, elected 1986)

Title: Primate of the Russian Orthodox Church Outside Russia

Residence: New York, New York, USA

MEMBERSHIP: 150,000

## III. D. 3. *The Ukrainian Autocephalous Orthodox Church*

Although the church in Kiev survived the Mongol destruction of the city in 1240, its metropolitans soon began to reside in the new principality of Moscow. This situation continued until 1448, when Kiev, then under Polish-Lithuanian domination, was established as a distinct metropolitanate under the jurisdiction of Constantinople. Soon thereafter, in 1461, the bishops of Moscow ceased using the title of Kiev and began to style themselves as Metropolitans of Moscow. Moscow later gathered strength and eventually gained control of Kiev. The Orthodox Metropolitanate of Kiev was consequently transferred from the jurisdiction of Constantinople to that of Moscow in 1686.

The Orthodox Church in the Ukraine thus was part of the Russian Orthodox Church until the independence of the Ukraine was declared in the chaotic situation following World War I and the Russian revolution. The government of this new republic passed a law allowing for the establishment of an autocephalous Ukrainian Orthodox Church in 1919.

Meanwhile, a spontaneous movement began among Ukrainian Orthodox which established an autocephalous Orthodox Church at a council which met in 1920. But no Orthodox bishop would take part in this action, so the council decided to ordain a bishop through the laying-on-of-hands by the priests and laypeople present. Because of this highly unorthodox procedure for ordaining its first bishop, and because of its disregard for some established canonical principles, this church has never been recognized by any other Orthodox Church. Strong lay participation in the this church's administration caused it to become known as the "sobornopravna" or "conciliar" church.

When the Ukraine was absorbed into the Soviet Union, the new authorities at first viewed the Ukrainian Orthodox Church in a positive way, but by the late 1920's, they saw it as a dangerous expression of Ukrainian nationalism. Under government pressure, it declared itself dissolved and integrated into the Moscow Patriarchate in 1930.

However, during the German occupation of the Ukraine during World War II, the Ukrainian Orthodox Church was briefly reestablished by bishops who had been validly ordained by Polish Orthodox bishops. Thus it has subsequently claimed to be within the traditional apostolic succession, a fact still disputed by some Orthodox churches. In any case, it was suppressed again when the Soviets regained control of the area. The head of the church took up residence in exile in the United States. This remained the situation until greater religious freedom began to be established in the Soviet Union.

In these new conditions, a Ukrainian Orthodox council met in Kiev in June 1990 and elected the exiled Metropolitan Mstyslav as Patriarch. He returned to Ukraine in October 1990 to preside over the reemergence of this church in its homeland.

The situation became more complicated after 21 May 1992, when the Moscow Patriarchate deposed Metropolitan Filaret of Kiev, and reduced him to the lay state on June 11. He had been accused of

trying to separate his church from Moscow. Filaret then joined forces
with the autocephalous Ukrainian Orthodox Church and even took
the title of *locum tenens* of Patriarch Mstyslav who had returned to
the United States. Filaret enjoyed the support of the Ukrainian government in his efforts to form an autocephalous Orthodox Church.
All this happened, however, without the knowledge of Patriarch
Mstyslav who broke all ties with Filaret in November. This provoked
a split within the autocephalous church between those loyal to
Mstyslav and those linked to Filaret, who now call themselves "The
Ukrainian Orthodox Church-Kiev Patriarchate" (UOC-KP). After
Patriarch Mstyslav died on June 11, 1993, each of these two groups
elected its own head. Archbishop Petro of Lviv was chosen to lead
the bishops who had been loyal to Mstyslav, while the UOC-KP
chose Archbishop Volodymyr Romaniuk of Lviv and Sokal as acting
primate until the election of a new Patriarch at an "All-Ukrainian
Orthodox Sobor," which was to be held on October 21st. At this
writing it was not clear whether the bishops in communion with
Archbishop Petro would participate in the meeting. Meanwhile, the
church in the United States changed its name to "The Ukrainian
Orthodox Church in the USA" and was maintaining neutrality in the
dispute.

The Ukrainian Autocephalous Orthodox Church has a significant
presence in the diaspora. Beginning in the 19th century, large
numbers of Ukrainian immigrants in the United States and Canada
had integrated with Russian Orthodox parishes there. There were
also several waves of conversions of Greek Catholics to Orthodoxy.
By the 1920's, with nationalistic feelings intensified by events in the
Ukraine, groups in the United States (1919-1920) and Canada (1918),
and later in Western Europe, declared themselves to be part of the
new autocephalous Ukrainian Orthodox Church.

Distinct jurisdictions exist in the United States and Western
Europe. Another in Canada has recently been received under the
jurisdiction of the Ecumenical Patriarchate [see III.C.6]. The church
in the United States has just over 100 parishes, and is headed by
Metropolitan Constantine (PO Box 495, South Bound Brook, New
Jersey 08880). Ukrainian Orthodox in Great Britain are under the care

of Bishop Ioan Derevjanka whose offices are at 1A Newton Avenue, Acton, London W3 8AJ. The President of the Ukrainian Orthodox Consistory of Australia and New Zealand is Very Rev. Mykola Serdiuk, 21 Timbury Street, Moorooka, Queensland 4105.

LOCATION: Ukraine, USA, Western Europe

HEAD: vacant

MEMBERSHIP: 255,000 plus an undetermined number in Ukraine

## III. D. 4. The Belarusian Autocephalous Orthodox Church

Belarus (formerly known as Byelorussia or "White Russia") was for many centuries a part of the Russian Empire and later the Soviet Union. When with Russia, this region's mostly Orthodox population has always been part of the Russian Orthodox Church.

When Moscow's authority was weakened because of the chaos which followed the 1917 revolution, an unsuccessful attempt was made in 1922 to establish an autocephalous Belarusian Orthodox Church. Under Nazi occupation during the Second World War, the Germans supported both the revival of religious practice and the creation of separate Orthodox churches in order to weaken the allegiance of local populations to Moscow. Under strong Nazi pressure, a group of Belarusian Orthodox bishops declared the Belarusian Church autocephalous in 1942, but this status was ended when the Soviets reoccupied the area.

These bishops then emigrated to the west, and joined the Russian Orthodox Church Outside Russia. But in 1949, a group of Belarusian bishops in exile declared themselves autocephalous. Thus this group exists only in the diaspora, and has not been recognized by any Orthodox church. It has not reestablished itself in Belarus following that country's independence in 1991.

After the death of Archbishop Andrei Kryt in the late 1970's, there was a split in the Belarusian Orthodox community, which now includes about 20 parishes worldwide. The two groups are led by Archbishop Michael Maciukevich (524 St. Clerens Avenue, Toronto, Ontario M6H 3W7, Canada) and Metropolitan Iziasłau Brucki (401

Atlantic Avenue, Brooklyn, New York 11217 USA). The community in Australia may be reached through Fr. Alexander Kulakouski, 42 Thornton Drive, St. Albans VIC 3021.

There are also four Belarusian Orthodox parishes in the United States and one in Canada under the jurisdiction of the Ecumenical Patriarchate [see III.C.5].

LOCATION: Diaspora
MEMBERSHIP: 140,000

## III. D. 5. The Macedonian Orthodox Church

Macedonia, an important geopolitical center of the Balkans since ancient times, has for centuries been a focal point of territorial rivalries involving Turkey, Serbia, Bulgaria, and Greece.

While Macedonia was under Ottoman administration, the Orthodox church there was part of the Patriarchate of Constantinople. When Turkish rule was ended following the Balkan Wars of 1912-1913, southern Macedonia became part of Greece. But northern Macedonia, inhabited by Slavs who called themselves Macedonians because of the name of the area in which they lived, was incorporated into the newly-formed kingdom of Yugoslavia. By agreement with the Ecumenical Patriarchate, the Orthodox in this northern area were integrated into the Serbian Patriarchate and reorganized into three dioceses.

When the communists took power in Yugoslavia following World War II, they decided to reorganize Yugoslavia on a federal basis, and provided for the creation of a separate Macedonian Republic. The communists supported the aspirations of some Macedonians who wished to assert their separate identity, in order to gain their backing for the new government.

During the same period, the government supported efforts by some Orthodox in the Macedonian Republic to establish a separate Macedonian Orthodox Church. In October 1958 an Ecclesiastical and National Council of 220 priests and laity was held in Ohrid which declared the restoration of the ancient Archbishopric of Ohrid, and the autonomy of the Macedonian Orthodox Church. It also elected three new bishops for the three dioceses of the church. This was considered an irregular election, as only one bishop was present. But the new church declared itself in canonical unity with the Serbian Orthodox Church in the person of the Serbian Patriarch. In June 1959 the Serbian Holy Synod accepted this *fait accompli*, and the next month the three bishops-elect were consecrated by Serbian Orthodox bishops.

In the autumn of 1966, the Macedonian Orthodox Church formally petitioned the Serbian Patriarchate for autocephalous status. But when it met in May 1967, the Serbian episcopate rejected this request.

Nevertheless, the Macedonians went forward and held a council in Ohrid on 17-19 July 1967. On July 19, acting on a resolution of the council, the Holy Synod of the Church of Macedonia proclaimed the autocephaly of the Orthodox Church in the Republic of Macedonia. The Metropolitan was given the new title of "Archbishop of Ohrid and Macedonia." All this was openly supported by the state authorities, who gave the new Metropolitan state honors and attended his installation ceremonies.

In September 1967 the Serbian Orthodox Synod declared the Macedonian Orthodox Church to be a schismatic religious organization, and broke off all liturgical and canonical links with its hierarchy, although not with its faithful. This decision has been supported by other Orthodox Churches, as none has recognized the legitimacy of this Macedonian Church.

The disintegration of Yugoslavia led to Macedonia's declaration of independence in 1991. But its name has been disputed by Greece and consequently it has not been recognized by most of the countries of the world.

In December 1991 Archbishop Gavril resigned his post as head of the church, possibly because of tensions within the hierarchy concerning the church's canonical status. But he was persuaded to withdraw his resignation after the Holy Synod assured him of its confidence. Serbian Patriarch Pavle received a delegation of Macedonian Orthodox bishops in mid-1992 to discuss the church's status, but so far these contacts have not led to a restoration of canonical communion. Indeed, the appointment of a bishop for Macedonia by the Serbian Orthodox Church seems to have intensified the dispute.

At the time of the declaration of autocephaly in 1967, the Macedonian Orthodox Church included some 334 priests ministering in approximately 400 parishes. Monasticism has experienced a serious decline. In 1992 it was reported that there were a total of ten religious sisters associated with communities in Bitola and Prilep, while a young religious community of men had been founded at the ancient monastery of Saint Naum on Lake Ohrid.

Macedonian Orthodox bishops resident in Skopje, the republic's capital, have responsibility for the Macedonian parishes in the diaspora which have adhered to this church. Metropolitan Stefan is responsible for the United States and Canada where there are about 20 parishes, while Bishop Timotei oversees the 18 parishes and two monasteries in Australia.

> LOCATION: Former Yugoslav Republic of Macedonia, diaspora in North America and Australia
> HEAD: Archbishop Gavril (born 1912, elected 1986)
> Title: Archbishop of Ohrid and Macedonia
> Residence: Skopje, Former Yugoslav Republic of Macedonia
> MEMBERSHIP: 1,200,000

## III. D. 6. The Old Calendar Orthodox Churches in Greece and Romania

After the turn of the century various Orthodox Churches, beginning with the Patriarchate of Constantinople, began to abandon the old Julian calendar for some purposes and adopt the new Gregorian calendar, which is about 12 days ahead of the Julian. At present most Orthodox Churches (with the exception of Jerusalem, Russia, Serbia, and Mount Athos) use the new calendar for fixed feasts, but the Julian calendar for Easter and movable feasts dependent upon it.

This reform was introduced in the Church of Greece in 1924 by the Holy Synod with support from the government. However, strong opposition was immediately expressed, mainly among the lower clergy and laity. This group claimed that such a decision could only be taken by an ecumenical council in which the entire Orthodox Church would be involved. Three Greek Orthodox bishops supported them and threatened schism.

In 1935 the Holy Synod of the Church of Greece deposed the three bishops, deprived them of episcopal rank, and sentenced them to five years of seclusion in a monastery. The Holy Synod also asked the government to either use effective means to suppress the opposition or agree to a restoration of the Julian calendar. The authorities refused to take decisive action, however, in part because most of those opposed to the reforms supported the monarchy which was weak at the time.

Those opposed to the new calendar became known as the "Old Calendarists," or "Church of True Orthodox Christians of Greece." In the early years they were led by Metropolitan Chrysostomos of Florina. The community was also plagued by divisions, usually over the question of the validity of the sacraments of the Orthodox Church of Greece. A smaller group insisted that there was no such grace in the sacraments of the official church. After the death of Chrysostomos in 1955, the church was left without bishops. But in 1960 new bishops were consecrated for it by bishops of the Russian Orthodox Church Outside Russia. New divisions occurred in the 1970's, causing the movement to split into several hostile camps.

Although the Old Calendarists were actively persecuted in Greece especially during the 1950's, today they are allowed to function freely. They claim to have hundreds of thousands of faithful in Greece, over 200 priests, and almost 100 monastic communities in the Athens area. Their churches are recognizable by the absence of electric lighting and pews, and their practices include traditional Byzantine chant and frequent all-night vigils. A small ultra-extremist minority known as "Matthewites" have about 40 priests in Greece and a strong monastic tradition centered on the convent of the Entrace of the Theotokos at Keratea (300 nuns) and Transfiguration Monastery (60 monks). Their several tens of thousands of faithful firmly believe that they are the only Orthodox left in the world.

Greek Old Calendarist sources claim that in the United States in 1991 there were probably about 30 parishes belonging to the one of the jurisdictions in Greece, at least four monasteries or convents and perhaps as many as 15,000 faithful. There are four parishes in Australia.

A parallel development took place in Romania after Patriarch Miron Cristea introduced the Gregorian calendar in 1924. Opposition centered around the abbot of Pokrov Skete in Moldavia, Hieromonk Glicherie. By 1936 he had built 40 churches, most of them in Moldavia. The Romanian government took strong measures against the movement so that by the eve of World War II, all the Old Calendar churches had been closed. But after the war Glicherie resumed his efforts and by 1950 nearly all these churches had been reopened.

The communists allowed the movement to continue, although they subjected it to periodic persecutions. In 1955 a retired Romanian Orthodox bishop, Metropolitan Galaction Cordun, joined the Old Calendarists and began ordaining priests for them. He also single-handedly ordained three new bishops, thus establishing a continuing hierarchy. The community has not experienced the divisions that have troubled the Old Calendar Church in Greece, with which it is in communion.

Today the Romanian Old Calendar Church claims to have 500,000 believers with eight large monasteries. Since 1990 construction has begun on 60 new churches. The first hierarch, Metropolitan Vlasie (elected 1992) resides at Holy Transfiguration Monastery at Slatioara, the spiritual and administrative center of the church.

## IV. The Catholic Eastern Churches

The split between the Latin and Byzantine Churches, which had been symbolized by the mutual excommunications of the bishops of Rome and Constantinople in 1054, became definitive in the minds of the common people in the east after the Crusades and the sacking of Constantinople by the Latins in 1204. Attempts at reunion took place at the Second Council of Lyons in 1274 and at the Council of Ferrara-Florence in 1439, but neither was successful.

Subsequently, a Roman Catholic theology of the Church continued to develop which vigorously emphasized the necessity of the direct jurisdiction of the Pope over all the local churches. This implied that churches not under the Pope's jurisdiction could be considered objects of missionary activity for the purpose of bringing them into communion with the Roman Catholic Church. At the same time, the notion of "rite" developed, according to which groups of eastern Christians who came into union with Rome would be absorbed into the single Church, but allowed to maintain their own liturgical tradition and canonical discipline.

This missionary activity, which was sometimes carried out with the support of Catholic governments of countries with Orthodox minorities, was directed towards all the Eastern Churches. Eventually segments of virtually all of these churches came into union with Rome. It should be recognized, however, that not all these unions were the result of the activity of Catholic missionaries. The Bulgarian Byzantine Catholic Church, for example, was the direct result of a spontaneous movement of Orthodox towards Rome. And the Maronites in Lebanon claim never to have been out of communion with the Roman Church.

Inevitably, these unions resulted in a process of "latinization," or the adoption of certain practices and attitudes proper to the Latin Church, to a certain degree, depending on the circumstances of the group. As a result, these churches sometimes lost contact with their spiritual roots. The monastic tradition, so central to Orthodox spirituality, died out in most of the Eastern Catholic Churches, although religious life often continued in the form of congregations modeled on Latin apostolic communities.

All of these churches come under the jurisdiction of the Pope through the Sacred Congregation for the Oriental Churches, one of the offices of the Roman Curia. It was created in 1862 as part of the *Propaganda Fide*, and was made an autonomous Congregation by Benedict XV in 1917. It has the same role with regard to bishops, clergy, religious, and the faithful in the Eastern Catholic Churches that other offices of the Curia have in relation to the Latin Church. The Oriental Congregation also oversees the prestigious Pontifical Oriental Institute in Rome, which is under the direction of the Jesuits and has one of the best libraries for Eastern Christian studies in the world.

It should be mentioned that the expression "uniate," often used in the past to describe the Eastern Catholic Churches, is now generally considered derogatory, and consequently is falling into disuse.

Most Orthodox view these churches as an obstacle in the way of reconciliation between the Catholic and Orthodox Churches. They feel that their very existence constitutes a denial by Catholics of the ecclesial reality of the Orthodox churches, and that these unions grew from efforts to split local Orthodox communities. They tend to consider Eastern Catholics either as Orthodox whose presence in the Catholic Church is an abnormal situation brought about by coercive measures, or even as Roman Catholics pretending to be Orthodox for the purpose of proselytism.

One of the documents of the Second Vatican Council, *Orientalium Ecclesiarum*, dealt with the Eastern Catholic Churches. It affirmed their equality with the Latin Church, and called upon Eastern Catholics to rediscover their authentic traditions. It also affirmed that Eastern Catholics have a special vocation to foster ecumenical relations with the Orthodox.

The ecclesial life of the Eastern Catholic Churches is governed in accordance with the *Code of Canons of the Eastern Churches* which was promulgated by Pope John Paul II on 18 October 1990 and began to have the force of law on 1 October 1991. According to the new

Oriental Code, the Eastern Catholic Churches fall into four categories: 1. Patriarchal (the Chaldean, Armenian, Coptic, Syrian, Maronite, and Melkite Churches), 2. Major Archepiscopal (Ukrainian and Syro-Malabar Catholic Churches), 3. Metropolitan *sui iuris* (the Ethiopian, Syro-Malankara, Romanian and American Ruthenian Churches), and 4. other churches *sui iuris* (Bulgarian, Greek, Hungarian, Italo-Albanian, and Slovak Churches, as well as a diocese covering all of former Yugoslavia). The Belarusian, Albanian, Georgian and Russian Eastern Catholic Churches have no hierarchy.

Eastern Catholic Patriarchs are elected by the Synod of Bishops of that particular church. The one elected Patriarch is immediately proclaimed and enthroned. He subsequently requests ecclesiastical communion from the Pope. The synods of patriarchal churches also elect bishops for dioceses within the patriarchal territory from a list of candidates that have been approved by the Holy See. If the one elected has not been previously approved, he must obtain the consent of the Pope before ordination as bishop. A Major Archbishop is elected in the same manner as a Patriarch, but his election must be confirmed by the Roman Pontiff before he can be enthroned. Metropolitans are named by the Pope on the basis of a list of at least three candidates submitted by the council of bishops of that particular church.

In the presentation which follows, the Eastern Catholic Churches are grouped according to their provenance. It begins with those which have no direct non-Catholic counterpart, and then considers the Eastern Catholic Churches which correspond to the Assyrian Church of the East, the Oriental Orthodox, and, finally, the Orthodox Churches.

## The Congregation for the Oriental Churches
Achille Cardinal Silvestrini, Prefect
(born 1923, ordained bishop 1979, Cardinal 1988, Prefect 1991)
Archbishop Miroslav Stefan Marusyn, Secretary
Via della Conciliazione, 34
00120 Vatican City State

## IV. A. Churches With No Direct Counterpart

These are two Eastern Catholic churches which, because of unique historical circumstances, do not have an immediate counterpart among the other Eastern Churches.

## IV. A. 1. The Maronite Catholic Church

The Maronites of Lebanon trace their origin back to the late 4th century when a group of disciples gathered around the charismatic figure Saint Maron. They later founded a monastery located midway between Aleppo and Antioch. Although it was within the Antiochene Patriarchate, the community developed its own distinct traditions. In the 5th century the monastery vigorously supported the christological doctrine of the Council of Chalcedon.

By the 8th century, the monks had moved with their band of followers into the remote mountains of Lebanon where they existed in relative isolation for centuries. It was also during this period that they began to develop a distinct identity as a church, and to elect a bishop as their head, who took the title of Patriarch of Antioch and All the East.

The Maronites came into contact with the Latin Church in the 12th century, when the Latin Crusader Kingdom of Antioch was founded. In 1182 the entire Maronite nation formally confirmed its union with Rome. But there is a strong tradition among the Maronites that their church never lacked communion with the Holy See.

Patriarch Jeremias II Al-Amshitti (1199-1230) became the first Maronite Patriarch to visit Rome when he attended the fourth Lateran council there in 1215. This marked the beginning of close relations with the Holy See and a continuing latinizing tendency. The 16th century also saw the conquest of the Maronite homeland by the Turks and the beginning of long centuries of Ottoman domination.

By the 19th century the western powers, especially France, began to offer protection to the Maronites within the Ottoman Empire. A massacre of thousands of them in 1860 provoked intervention by French military forces. After World War I both Lebanon and Syria came under French control.

When France granted Lebanon full independence in 1944, it attempted to guarantee the safety of the Maronite community by leaving behind a constitution guaranteeing that there would always be a Maronite President. The civil war which erupted in Lebanon in 1975 revealed, however, that the community's future remained precarious. Indeed, many thousands of Maronites have been leaving Lebanon to make new lives for themselves in the west.

The Maronite Patriarch has resided at Bkerke, about 25 miles from Beirut, since 1790. Today there are ten dioceses in Lebanon with about 850 parishes, and six other jurisdictions in the Middle East. This is the largest church in Lebanon, making up about 37% of the Christians and 17% of the overall population.

There is a Maronite Patriarchal Seminary at Ghazir and a diocesan seminary at Karm Sadde, near Tripoli. Advanced theological education is provided at the University of the Holy Spirit at Kaslik. A Maronite College was founded in Rome in 1584.

The Maronite liturgy is of West Syrian origin, but it has been influenced by the East Syrian and Latin traditions. The Eucharist is essentially a variation of the Syriac liturgy of St. James. Originally celebrated in Syriac, the liturgy has been for the most part in Arabic since the Arab invasions.

The steady emigration of Maronites from Lebanon in recent years has produced flourishing communities in the diaspora. In the United States, the diocese of St. Maron of Brooklyn, presided over by Archbishop Francis Zayek (8120 15th Avenue, Brooklyn, New York 11228) has 60 parishes and 53,222 members. In Canada, the diocese of St. Maron of Montreal, headed by Bishop George Abi-Saber (12475 Grenet Street, Montreal, Quebec H4J 2K4) has only nine parishes but about 80,000 faithful. Bishop Joseph Hitti oversees the diocese of St. Maron of Sydney (105 The Boulevard, P.O. Box 385, Strathfield, NSW

2135 Australia), which has 10 parishes for an estimated 150,000 Maronites in Australia.

LOCATION: Lebanon, Syria, Cyprus, Egypt, Brazil, USA, Canada, Australia

HEAD: Patriarch Nasrallah Sfeir (born 1920, elected 1986)

Title: Patriarch of Antioch of the Maronites

Residence: Bkerke, Lebanon

MEMBERSHIP: 3,303,000

## IV. A. 2. The Italo-Albanian Catholic Church

Southern Italy and Sicily had a strong connection with Greece in antiquity and for many centuries there was a large Greek-speaking population there. In the early centuries of the Christian era, although most of the Christians were of the Byzantine tradition, the area was included in the Roman Patriarchate, and a gradual but incomplete process of latinization began.

During the 8th century, Byzantine Emperor Leo III removed this region from papal jurisdiction and placed it within the Patriarchate of Constantinople. There followed a strong revival of the Byzantine tradition in the area. But the Norman conquest in the early 11th century resulted in its return to the Latin Patriarchate. By this time the local Byzantine church was flourishing, and there were hundreds of monasteries along the coasts of southern Italy. The Normans, however, discouraged Byzantine usages in their lands, and the Greek bishops were replaced by Latin ones. This marked the beginning of a process which led to the almost total absorption of the Byzantine faithful into the Latin Church.

This decline was reversed in the 15th century with the arrival of two large groups of Albanian immigrants who had fled their country following its conquest by the Turks. Those from the northern part of Albania, where the Latin rite was prevalent, were quickly absorbed into the local population. But those from the Orthodox south of the country remained loyal to their Byzantine traditions. At first they met with little understanding from the local Latin bishops. Although in the 16th century Popes intervened in favor of the Byzantines — in 1595 an ordaining bishops was appointed for them — the community continued to decline.

The situation began to improve in the 18th century. In 1742 Pope Benedict XIV published the bull *Etsi pastoralis* which was intended to buttress the position of the Italo-Albanians in relation to the Latins. It paved the way for more progressive legislation — and recognition of the equality of the Byzantine rite with the Latin — in the next century.

Italo-Albanian seminaries were founded in 1732 in Calabria and in 1734 in Palermo. Seminarians in advanced theological studies in Rome reside at the Greek College (founded in 1577).

Today there are two dioceses for the Italo-Albanians of equal rank: the diocese of Lungro (in Calabria) was founded in 1919, has 27 parishes, and has jurisdiction over continental Italy. The diocese of Piana degli Albanesi, founded in 1937, covers all of Sicily and has 15 parishes. Alongside these two dioceses is the monastery of Santa Maria di Grottaferrata, just a few miles from Rome, which, having been founded in the 11th century, is the only remnant of the once-flourishing Italo-Greek monastic tradition. Since 1937 the abbot has been a bishop with jurisdiction over the monks of the monastery and local faithful.

Most Italo-Albanians in the diaspora have been absorbed into local Latin parishes. They have no parishes in the United States, but the community's identity has been preserved through such groups as the Italo-Albanian Byzantine Rite Society of Our Lady of Grace based in Staten Island, New York.

LOCATION: Southern Italy, small diaspora
MEMBERSHIP: 62,000

## IV. B. *From The Assyrian Church Of The East*

### IV. B. 1. *The Chaldean Catholic Church*

As early as the 13th century, Catholic missionaries — primarily Dominicans and Franciscans — had been active among the faithful of the Assyrian Church of the East [see I]. This resulted in a series of individual conversions of bishops and brief unions, but no permanent community was formed.

In the mid-15th century a tradition of hereditary patriarchal succession (passing from uncle to nephew) took effect in the Assyrian Church. As a result, one family dominated the church and untrained minors were being elected to the patriarchal throne.

When such a patriarch was elected in 1552, a group of Assyrian bishops refused to accept him and decided to seek union with Rome. They elected the reluctant abbot of a monastery, Yuhannan Sulaka, as their own patriarch and sent him to Rome to arrange a union with the Catholic Church. In early 1553 Pope Julius III proclaimed him Patriarch Simon VIII "of the Chaldeans" and ordained him a bishop in St. Peter's Basilica on April 9, 1553.

The new Patriarch returned to his homeland in late 1553, and began to initiate a series of reforms. But opposition, led by the rival Assyrian Patriarch, was strong. Simon was soon captured by the pasha of Amadya, tortured and executed in January 1555. This began a long period of conflict between Chaldeans and Assyrians in which the Chaldeans eventually got the upper hand. It is now estimated that the Chaldean Catholic Church is three times as large as the Assyrian Church of the East.

The Chaldean Catholics suffered heavily from massacres during World War I (1918) when four bishops, many priests, and about 70,000 faithful died.

The location of the Patriarchate shifted back and forth among several places over the centuries, but gained a measure of stability after it was set up at Mosul in 1830. In 1950 it moved to its present location in Baghdad after substantial migration of Chaldean Catholics from northern Iraq to the capital city. Since the 19th century the Patriarch has had the title, "of Babylon of the Chaldeans."

Chaldean candidates for the priesthood study at St. Peter's Patriarchal Seminary in Baghdad. It no longer grants advanced degrees. There are centers offering courses in theology for the laity in Baghdad and Mosul. A proposal to set up a Catholic university in Iraq is being considered.

Today the largest concentration of members of these Catholics is in Baghdad, Iraq. There are ten Chaldean dioceses in Iraq, four in Iran, and five others in the Middle East. The Chaldean (or East Syrian) liturgy is in use, with the addition of a number of Latin customs. The liturgical language is Syriac.

The approximately 60,000 Chaldeans in the United States have 12 parishes in the diocese of St. Thomas the Apostle of Detroit of the Chaldeans, under the leadership of Bishop Ibrahim Ibrahim (25585 Berg Road, Southfield, Michigan 48034). In other areas of the diaspora, Chaldeans are under spiritual supervision of the local Latin ordinaries. In Australia the Catholic Chaldean Chaplain can be reached at 564 Sydney Road, Coburg VIC 3058.

LOCATION: Iraq, Iran, Syria, Lebanon, Turkey, Israel, Egypt, France, USA

HEAD: Patriarch Raphael I Bidawid (born 1922, elected 1989)

Title: Patriarch of Babylon of the Chaldeans

Residence: Baghdad, Iraq

MEMBERSHIP: 634,000

## IV. B. 2. The Syro-Malabar Catholic Church

Members of this church are directly descended from the Thomas Christians that the Portuguese encountered in 1498 while exploring the Malabar coast of India (now the state of Kerala). As mentioned above [see I: *Thomas Christians*], they were in full communion with the Assyrian Church in Persia. But they greeted the Portuguese as fellow Christians and as representatives of the Church of Rome, whose special status they had continued to acknowledge despite centuries of isolation.

It was difficult, however, for the Portuguese to accept the legitimacy of local Malabar traditions, and they began to impose Latin usages upon the Thomas Christians. At a synod held at Diamper in 1599 under the presidency of the Portuguese Archbishop of Goa, a number of such latinizations were adopted, including the appointment of Portuguese bishops, changes in the Eucharistic liturgy, the use of Roman vestments, the requirement of clerical celibacy, and the setting up of the Inquisition. This provoked widespread discontent which finally culminated in a decision by most Malabars in 1653 to break with Rome. In response, Pope Alexander VII sent Carmelite friars to Malabar to deal with the situation. By 1662 the majority of the dissidents had returned to communion with the Roman Catholic Church.

European Carmelites would continue to serve as bishops in the Syro-Malabar Church until 1896, when the Holy See established three Vicariates Apostolic for the Thomas Christians (Trichur, Ernakulam and Changanacherry), under the guidance of indigenous Syro-Malabar bishops. A fourth Vicariate Apostolic (Kottayam) was established in 1911. In 1923 Pope Pius XI set up a full-fledged the Syro-Malabar Catholic hierarchy.

This new autonomy initiated a strong revival of the church. While in 1876 there were approximately 200,000 Syro-Malabar Catholics, this number had more than doubled by 1931. By 1960 there were nearly 1½ million faithful, and today they number more than three million. Vocations to the priesthood have been very strong, and the church has about 21,000 religious women belonging to 16 different congregations, five of pontifical right. There are major seminaries at Alwaye (interritual), Kottayam, Satna, Bangalore, and Ujjain.

In 1934 Pope Pius XI initiated a process of liturgical reform in view of a restoration of the oriental nature of the heavily latinized Syro-Malabar rite. A restored eucharistic liturgy, drawing on the original East Syrian sources, was approved by Pius XIII in 1957 and introduced in 1962. Despite a reaffirmation of the main lines of the 1962 rite by the Oriental Congregation in 1985, however, there has been strong resistance to this reform. The majority of Syro-Malabar dioceses still use a rite which in externals is hardly distinguishable from the Latin Mass.

Relations between the Syro-Malabar Catholic Church and the Latin Church in India have often been marked by tension, particularly regarding the question of the establishment of Syro-Malabar jurisdictions in other parts of India to care for the many Malabars who have emigrated there. In 1987 the Holy See began to establish Syro-Malabar dioceses throughout India, even where Latin dioceses already exist.

Until 1993 there was no single head of the Syro-Malabar Catholic Church, but two metropolitan dioceses (Ernakulam and Changanacherry) of equal rank. But on 29 January of that year Pope John Paul II raised it to the rank of a Major Archepiscopal Church. He appointed Cardinal Antony Padiyara as Major Archbishop, but confided the pastoral government of the church to a Pontifical Delegate in the person of Archbishop Abraham Kattumana.

LOCATION: India, especially Kerala State

HEAD: Antony Cardinal Padiyara

Title: Major Archbishop of Ernakulam-Angamaly

Residence: Ernakulam, India

MEMBERSHIP: 3,037,000

## IV. C. From The Oriental Orthodox Churches

### IV. C. 1. The Armenian Catholic Church

The Latin Crusaders established close contacts with the Armenian Apostolic Church in the 12th century when they passed through the Armenian kingdom in Cilicia on their way to the Holy Land. An alliance between the Crusaders and the Armenian king contributed to the establishment of a union between the two churches in Cilicia in 1198. This union, which was not accepted by Armenians outside

Cilicia, ended with the conquest of the Armenian kingdom by the Tatars in 1375.

A decree of reunion with the Armenian Apostolic Church, *Exultate Deo*, was published at the Council of Florence on 22 November 1439. Although it had no immediate results, the document provided the doctrinal basis for the establishment of an Armenian Catholic Church much later.

Catholic missionary activity among the Armenians had begun early, led initially by the Friars of Union, a now-defunct Armenian community, related to the Dominicans, founded in 1320. With the passage of time, scattered but growing Armenian Catholic communities began to ask for a proper ecclesial structure and their own patriarch. In 1742 Pope Benedict XIV confirmed a former Armenian Apostolic bishop, Abraham Ardzivian (1679-1749) as Patriarch of Cilicia of the Armenians, based in Lebanon, and with religious authority over the Armenian Catholics in the southern provinces of the Ottoman Empire. In the north, they continued to be under the spiritual care of the Latin Vicar Apostolic in Constantinople. The new patriarch took the name Abraham Pierre I, and all his successors have likewise taken the name Pierre in their ecclesiastical title.

The Ottoman millet system, which provided for the administrative autonomy of minorities under the direction of their religious leaders, had placed all Armenian Catholics under the civil jurisdiction of the Armenian Apostolic Patriarch in Constantinople. This resulted in serious difficulties for Armenian Catholics and even persecutions until 1829 when, under French pressure, the Ottoman government gave them the right to be organized civilly as a separate millet, with an Archbishop of their own in Constantinople. In 1846 he was vested with civil authority as well. The anomaly of having an Archbishop with both civil and religious authority in the Ottoman capital and an exclusively spiritual Patriarch in Lebanon was resolved in 1867 when Pope Pius IX united the two sees and moved the patriarchal residence to Constantinople.

The vicious persecution of Armenians in Turkey at the end of World War I decimated the Armenian Catholic community in that country: seven bishops, 130 priests, 47 nuns and as many as 100,000 faithful died. Since the community in Turkey had been drastically reduced in size, an Armenian Catholic synod in Rome in 1928 decided to transfer the Patriarchate back to Lebanon (Beirut), and to make Constantinople (now Istanbul) an Archbishopric.

There were also a number of Armenian Catholic communities in the section of historic Armenia which came under Russian control in 1828. Pius IX established the diocese of Artvin for all Armenian Catholics in the Russian Empire in 1850. But czarist opposition to Eastern-rite Catholicism resulted in the abandonment of the Artvin diocese within 40 years. In 1912 the Armenian Catholics in the Empire were placed under the Latin bishop of distant Tiraspol. The Armenian Catholic Church was entirely suppressed under communism, and it was only with the independence of Armenia in 1991 that communities of Armenian Catholics began to resurface. In October 1991 the Holy See established an Ordinariat for Armenian Catholics in Eastern Europe based in the new republic. And in November 1992 an Armenian Catholic synod took place in Rome to consider the church's needs in this new situation.

An important example of Armenian Catholic religious life is provided by the Mechitarist Fathers, founded in Constantinople in 1701. It transferred to the island of San Lazzaro, Venice, in 1717. In 1811 a second foundation of Mechitarists was set up in Vienna. These two communities have long served the entire Armenian nation through their scholarship both in Europe and the Middle East.

A brotherhood of priests at Bzoummar, Lebanon, has an extensive library and a seminary that dates back to 1771. For higher theological studies, an Armenian College was founded in Rome in 1883.

Today the largest concentrations of Armenian Catholics are in Beirut, Lebanon, and Aleppo, Syria. The church has seven dioceses in the Middle East: two in Syria and one each in Lebanon, Iraq, Iran, Egypt and Turkey.

Armenian Catholics in Britain, Australia, and New Zealand are under the spiritual supervision of the local Latin ordinaries. There is an Armenian Chaplain for Australia at 41 Station Street, Ferntree Gully, VIC 3156. In the United States and Canada, however, the 39,000 Armenian Catholics form an apostolic exarchate of eight parishes under the direction of Bishop Mikail Nerses Setian (110 East 12th Street, New York, New York 10003).

LOCATION: Lebanon, Syria, Iraq, Turkey, Egypt, Iran, Diaspora
HEAD: Patriarch Jean Pierre XVIII Kasparian (born 1927, elected 1982)
Title: Patriarch of Cilicia of the Armenians
Residence: Beirut, Lebanon
MEMBERSHIP: 147,000

## IV. C. 2. The Coptic Catholic Church

A formal union between the Catholic and Coptic Orthodox Churches [see II.B] took place with the signing of the document *Cantate Domino* by a Coptic delegation at the Council of Florence on 4 February 1442. But, because this act was not supported in Egypt, it had no concrete results.

The first significant activity of Catholic missionaries among the Copts took place in the 17th century, with the Franciscans in the lead. A Capuchin mission was founded in Cairo in 1630, and in 1675 the Jesuits began missionary activity in Egypt. During the same century a number of lengthy but fruitless theological exchanges took place between Rome and the Coptic Church.

In 1741 a Coptic bishop in Jerusalem, Amba Athanasius, became a Catholic. Pope Benedict XIV appointed him Vicar Apostolic of the small community of Egyptian Coptic Catholics, which at that time numbered no more than 2,000. Although Athanasius eventually returned to communion with the Coptic Orthodox Church, a line of Catholic Vicars Apostolic continued after him.

In 1824, under the mistaken impression that the Ottoman viceroy wished it to do so, the Holy See erected a Patriarchate for Coptic Catholics, but for now it only existed on paper. The Ottoman authorities permitted the Coptic Catholics to begin building their own churches in 1829.

In 1895 Leo XIII re-established the Patriarchate, and in 1899 appointed Fr. Cyril Makarios as Patriarch Cyril II "of Alexandria of the

Copts." Cyril had presided over a Catholic Coptic synod in 1898 which introduced a number of Latin practices. But he became embroiled in controversy, and felt compelled to resign in 1908. The office remained vacant until 1947, when a new patriarch was finally elected and there began the line which continues today.

While the offices of the patriarchate are located in Cairo, the largest concentration of Coptic Catholics has always been in upper Egypt. In more recent times, however, there has been some migration to other parts of the country.

Most candidates for the priesthood are trained at St. Leo's Patriarchal Seminary in Maadi, a suburb of Cairo. There are also minor seminaries at Maadi, Tahta and Alexandria. More than 100 Coptic Catholic parishes administer primary schools, and some have secondary schools as well. The church maintains a hospital in Assuit, a number of medical dispensaries and clinics, and several orphanages.

There are no Coptic Catholic monasteries to rival the Coptic Orthodox monastic tradition, but there are religious orders modeled on western apostolic communities involved in educational, medical, and charitable activities.

In 1990 Coptic Catholic sources estimated that there were about 10,000 faithful in the diaspora under the care of local Latin bishops. There are a total of six parishes located in Paris (France), Montréal (Canada), Brooklyn and Los Angeles (USA), and Sydney and Melbourne (Australia).

LOCATION: Egypt
HEAD: Patriarch Stephanos II Ghattas (born 1920, elected 1986)
Title: Patriarch of Alexandria of the Copts
Residence: Cairo, Egypt
MEMBERSHIP: 182,000

## IV. C. 3. The Ethiopian Catholic Church

After some early unsuccessful missionary activity by Dominican friars, the Portuguese Jesuits became involved in a major effort in the

16th century to bring the Ethiopian Orthodox Church [see II.C] into union with Rome.

Largely through the efforts of Father Peter Paez, SJ, the Ethiopian negus (king) Susenyos became a Catholic and declared Roman Catholicism the state religion in 1622. In the following year, Pope Gregory XV appointed another Portuguese Jesuit, Affonso Mendez, as Patriarch of Ethiopia. Formal union of the two churches was proclaimed when Mendez arrived in Ethiopia in 1626.

However, Mendez imposed a series of latinizations on the Ethiopian liturgy, customs, and discipline, which Susenyos then tried to enforce with cruelty and bloodshed. This led to a violent public reaction. Susenyos died in 1632, and his successor was sympathetic to those who rejected the union. In 1636 Mendez was expelled, the union was dissolved, and many Catholic missionaries were put to death. The country was closed to Catholic missionary activity for 200 years.

In 1839 limited activity was resumed by the Lazarists and Capuchins, but public hostility was still very strong. It was only with the accession of King Menelik II to the throne in 1889 that Catholic missionaries could again work freely in the country. Catholic missionary activity expanded in Ethiopia during the Italian occupation from 1935 to 1941, as it had earlier in Eritrea which had been under Italian control since 1889.

The present ecclesiastical structure of the Ethiopian Catholic Church dates from 1961, when a metropolitan see was established at Addis Ababa with suffragan dioceses in Asmara and Adigrat. The largest concentrations of Ethiopian-rite Catholics are in Addis Ababa and Asmara. But with the independence of Eritrea on 24 May 1993, about half the faithful found themselves within that new country.

The Ethiopian Catholic Church maintains seminaries in each of the three dioceses. In 1919 Pope Benedict XV founded an Ethiopian College within the Vatican walls and restored St. Stephen's Church directly behind St. Peter's Basilica for the use of the college.

LOCATION: Ethiopia and Eritrea

HEAD: Cardinal Paulos Tzadua (born 1921, appointed 1977, cardinal 1985)

Title: Archbishop of Addis Ababa of the Ethiopians
Residence: Addis Ababa, Ethiopia
MEMBERSHIP: 133,000

## IV. C. 4. The Syrian Catholic Church

During the Crusades there were many examples of warm relationships between Catholic and Syrian Orthodox bishops. Some Syrian bishops seemed favorable to union with Rome, but no lasting results were achieved. There was also a decree of union between Syrian Orthodox and Rome at the Council of Florence, (*Multa et admirabilia* of 30 November 1444) but this also came to nothing.

Jesuit and Capuchin missionaries began to work among the Syrian Orthodox faithful at Aleppo in 1626. So many Syrians were received into communion with Rome that in 1662, when the Patriarchate had fallen vacant, the Catholic party was able to elect one of its own, Andrew Akhidjan, as Patriarch. This provoked a split in the community, and after Akhidjan's death in 1677 two opposed patriarchs were elected, an uncle and nephew, representing the two parties. But when the Catholic Patriarch died in 1702, this brief line of Syrian Catholic Patriarchs died out with him.

The Ottoman government supported the Oriental Orthodox against the Catholics, and throughout the 18th century the Catholic Syrians underwent much suffering and persecution. There were long periods when no Syrian Catholic bishops were functioning, and the community was forced underground.

In 1782 the Syrian Orthodox Holy Synod elected Metropolitan Michael Jarweh of Aleppo as Patriarch. But shortly after he was enthroned, he declared himself Catholic, took refuge in Lebanon and built the still-extant monastery of Our Lady at Sharfeh. After Jarweh there has been an unbroken succession of Syrian Catholic Patriarchs.

In 1829 the Turkish government granted legal recognition to the Syrian Catholic Church, and the residence of the Patriarch was established at Aleppo in 1831. Catholic missionary activity resumed. Because the Christian community at Aleppo had been severely persecuted, the Patriarchate was moved to Mardin (now in southern Turkey) in 1850.

Steady Syrian Catholic expansion at the expense of the Syrian Orthodox was ended by the persecutions and massacres which took place during World War I. In the early 1920's the Patriarchal residence was moved to Beirut, to which many Syrian Catholics had fled.

The Syrian Catholic Patriarch always takes the name Ignatius in addition to another name. Although Syrian Catholic priests were bound to celibacy at the Synod of Sharfeh in 1888, there are now a number of married priests. A patriarchal seminary and printing house are located at Sharfeh Monastery in Lebanon.

The largest concentrations of Syrian Catholics are found in Syria, Lebanon, and Iraq. Their common language is Arabic, but Syriac is still spoken in some villages in eastern Syria and northern Iraq. There are no Syrian Catholic bishops outside the Middle East.

LOCATION: Lebanon, Syria, Iraq
HEAD: Patriarch Ignatius Anthony II Hayek (born 1910, elected 1968)
Title: Patriarch of Antioch of the Syrians
Residence: Beirut, Lebanon
MEMBERSHIP: 104,000

## IV. C. 5. The Syro-Malankara Catholic Church

During the 18th century there were no less than four formal attempts to reconcile the Roman Catholic and Malankara Orthodox Syrian Churches [see II.E], all of which failed.

In 1926, a group of five Malankara Orthodox Syrian bishops who were opposed to the jurisdiction of the Syrian Orthodox Patriarch in India commissioned one of their own number, Mar Ivanios, to open negotiations with Rome with a view to reconciliation on the condition that their liturgy be preserved, and that the bishops be allowed to retain their dioceses. Rome asked that the bishops make a profession of faith, and that their baptisms and ordinations be proven valid in each case.

In the event, only two of the five bishops accepted the new arrangement with Rome, including Mar Ivanios, who had founded the first monastic communities for men and women in the Malankara Orthodox Syrian Church. These two bishops, a priest, a deacon and a layman were received into the Catholic Church together on 20 September 1930. Later in the 1930's two more bishops, from among those who had favored the jurisdiction of the Syrian Patriarch in India, were received into communion with Rome.

This triggered a significant movement of faithful into this new Syro-Malankara Catholic Church. By 1950 there were some 65,588 faithful, in 1960 112,478, and in 1970 183,490. There are now three dioceses for just over 280,000 faithful, all in Kerala State, India.

An interesting development in this church was the foundation of Kurisumala Ashram in 1958. This is a monastic community based on a strict Cistercian interpretation of the Benedictine monastic rule, the observance of the West Syrian liturgical tradition, and forms of asceticism in use among Hindu ascetics. It has become a spiritual center for Christians and Hindus alike.

In North America there are Malankara Catholic missions in Chicago, Dallas, Houston, New York, Philadelphia, Washington, and Toronto.

LOCATION: Kerala State, India

HEAD: Archbishop Benedict Mar Gregorios Thangalathil (born 1916, appointed 1955)

Title: Metropolitan of Trivandrum of the Syro-Malankarese

Residence: Trivandrum, Kerala State, India

MEMBERSHIP: 296,000


## IV. D. From The Orthodox Church

Before entering into full communion with Rome, all the churches in this section were part of the Orthodox Church. Because they retain the Byzantine Christian tradition, these churches are often described by the term "Byzantine Catholic" or "Greek Catholic."

## IV. D. 1. The Melkite Catholic Church

The word "Melkite" comes from the Syriac and Arabic words for "King," and was originally used to refer to those within the ancient Patriarchates of Alexandria, Antioch and Jerusalem [see III.A.2.3.4] who accepted the christological faith professed by the Byzantine Emperor after the Council of Chalcedon (451). Now, however, the term more often refers to Byzantine Catholics originating within those three Patriarchates.

Jesuits, Capuchins and Carmelites had been engaged in missionary activity in the Orthodox Patriarchate of Antioch since the mid-17th century. Although a number of these (including some bishops) formally entered the Catholic Church, by and large they remained mixed with Orthodox communities. Strictly speaking, the Melkite Catholic Church originated in a schism which took place within the Patriarchate of Antioch in the early 18th century. This division was exacerbated by a rivalry between the cities of Aleppo and Damascus.

Patriarch Athanasios III Debbas, who died on August 5, 1724, had designated as his successor a Cypriot monk named Sylvester. His candidacy was supported by the Aleppo party and the Patriarch of Constantinople. But on 20 September 1724 Damascene party elected as patriarch a strongly pro-Catholic man who took the name Cyril VI. A week later, the Patriarch of Constantinople ordained Sylvester as Patriarch of Antioch. The Ottoman government recognized Sylvester, while Cyril was deposed and excommunicated by Constantinople and compelled to seek refuge in Lebanon.

In 1729 Cyril's election as Patriarch of Antioch was recognized as valid by Pope Benedict XIII. But it was only in 1744 that Cyril was given the pallium as a sign of communion with Rome.

In the beginning this new Catholic community was limited to what is now Syria and Lebanon. But later Melkite Catholics began to immigrate to Palestine, and especially to Egypt after that country rebelled against Turkish control. For this reason the Melkite Catholic

Patriarch was given the additional titles of Patriarch of Jerusalem and Alexandria in 1838.

At first the Ottoman government had been very hostile to this new church and took strong measures against it. But conditions improved with the passage of time. In 1848 the government formally recognized the Melkite Catholic Church, and the Patriarchate itself moved to Damascus from Holy Savior Monastery near Sidon, Lebanon, where it had been established by Cyril VI after he fled there. This was followed by a period of growth, enhanced by the popular perception that the Melkite Church was becoming a focus of Arab resistance against the Turks. The Orthodox Patriarchate of Antioch, on the other hand, was viewed by many as dependent upon Constantinople and therefore upon the Ottoman government.

In the 19th century the Melkite Church experienced tensions in its relationship with Rome because many Melkites felt that their Byzantine identity was being threatened by those who favored greater integration into the Roman Catholic Church. This uneasiness was symbolized at Vatican I when Melkite Patriarch Gregory II Youssef voted against the constitution *Pastor Aeternus* which defined papal infallibility and universal jurisdiction.

At the Second Vatican Council, Melkite Patriarch Maximos IV Sayegh spoke forcefully against the latinization of the Eastern Catholic Churches, and urged a greater receptivity to the oriental Christian traditions, especially in the area of ecclesiology. Some Melkite bishops, including Patriarch Maximos IV, have supported the idea that, in the event of a reconciliation between the Orthodox and Catholic Churches, their church should be reintegrated into the Orthodox Patriarchate of Antioch.

St. Anne's Seminary in Jerusalem, under the direction of the White Fathers (now called the Missionaries of Africa), was the main seminary for the Melkite Church until it was closed in 1967 because of the political situation. Candidates for the priesthood now study at the patriarchal seminary of Raboué, Lebanon. Moreover, the Melkite Paulist Fathers direct an important theological institute at Harissa, and run a well known publishing house.

After the Maronites, the Melkite Catholic Church is the largest and most prosperous Catholic community in the Middle East. The majority its faithful is found in Syria, Lebanon, Israel and occupied territories, and Jordan.

Significant emigration from the Middle East in recent years has created flourishing Melkite communities in the West. The Diocese of Newton of the Melkites in the United States (19 Dartmouth Street, West Newton, Massachusetts 02165), currently without a bishop, has 44 parishes and 27,000 members. In Canada, the diocese of Saint-Sauveur de Montréal, under the guidance of Archbishop Michel Hakim (34 Maplewood, Outremont, Quebec H2V 2M1), has nine parishes and about 38,000 faithful. Archbishop George Riashi heads the diocese of Saint Michael's of Sydney in Australia (25 Golden Grove Street, Darlington, NSW 2008), which has eight parishes for 40,000 Melkite Catholics.

Location: Syria, Lebanon, Israel, Egypt, Jordan, the Americas, Europe, Australia

HEAD: Patriarch Maximos V Hakkim (born 1908, elected 1967)

Title: Greek Catholic Patriarch of Antioch and All the East, of Jerusalem, and of Alexandria

Residence: Damascus, Syria

MEMBERSHIP: 1,094,000

## IV. D. 2. The Ukrainian Catholic Church

The Ukrainians received the Christian faith in its Byzantine form, and their church was originally linked to the Patriarchate of Constantinople. But by the 14th century most Ukrainians were under the political control of Catholic Lithuania. Metropolitan Isidore of Kiev attended the Council of Florence and agreed to the 1439 act of union between Catholics and Orthodox. Although many Ukrainians within Lithuania initially accepted this union, within a few decades they had rejected it.

In 1569, Lithuania and Poland were united to form a single commonwealth, and most of Ukraine passed to Poland. By this time

Protestantism was expanding rapidly in the Ukrainian lands, and the Jesuits had begun to work for a local union between Catholics and Orthodox as a way of reducing Protestant influence. Soon many Orthodox also began to view such a union favorably as a way of improving the situation of the Ukrainian clergy, and of preserving their Byzantine traditions when Latin Polish Catholicism was expanding.

These developments culminated in a synod of Orthodox bishops at Brest in 1595-1596 which proclaimed a union between Rome and the Metropolitan province of Kiev. This event sparked a violent conflict between those who accepted the union and those opposed. The dioceses of the far western province of Galicia, which lie at the heart of what is now the Ukrainian Catholic Church, adhered to the union much later (Przemysl in 1692 and Lviv in 1700). By the 18th century, two-thirds of the Christians in western Ukraine had become Byzantine Catholic.

But as Orthodox Russia expanded its control into Ukraine, the union was gradually suppressed. In 1839, Czar Nicholas I abolished it in all areas under Russian rule with the exception of the eparchy of Kholm (in Polish territory) which was itself disbanded in 1875. Thus by the end of the 19th century Byzantine Catholicism had virtually disappeared from the empire.

But the Ukrainian Catholic Church survived in Galicia, which had come under Austrian rule in 1772 and passed to Poland at the end of World War I. The church flourished under the energetic leadership of Metropolitan Andrew Sheptyckyj, who was Archbishop of Lviv from 1900 to 1944. The situation changed dramatically, however, at the beginning of World War II, when most of Galicia was annexed by the Soviet Union.

The new Soviet administration acted decisively to liquidate the Ukrainian Catholic Church. In April 1945 all its bishops were arrested, and the following year they were sentenced to long terms of forced labor. In March 1946 a "synod" was held at Lviv which officially dissolved the union, and integrated the Ukrainian Catholic Church into the Russian Orthodox Church. Those who resisted were arrested, including over 1,400 priests and 800 nuns. Metropolitan

Joseph Slipyj, the head of the church, was sent to prison in Siberia. He was released in 1963 and exiled to Rome. In the same year he was given the title "Major Archbishop" of Lviv of the Ukrainians. He was made a cardinal in 1965 and died in 1984.

Although the exact role played by the Moscow Patriarchate in the suppression has not been clearly established, the events of 1946 poisoned the atmosphere between Ukrainian Catholics and Orthodox. All this came to the surface in the late 1980's when new religious freedoms inaugurated by Soviet President Michael Gorbachev enabled the Ukrainian Catholic Church to emerge from the catacombs.

On 1 December 1989 Ukrainian Catholic communities were given the right to register with the government. With the support of the local authorities, Ukrainian Catholics gradually began to take possession of their former churches. All this marked the beginning of a strong Ukrainian Catholic resurgence in the region. As this was happening, the Moscow Patriarchate protested that violence had been used in repossessing some churches (a claim the Catholics denied), and that Ukrainian Catholics were attempting to expand at the expense of the Orthodox. A series of high-level contacts between the Vatican and the Moscow Patriarchate began in 1990, but the talks have not yet been able to resolve the dispute satisfactorily.

In March 1991 Myroslav Ivan Cardinal Lubachivsky, the exiled head of the Ukrainian Catholic Church, was able to leave Rome and take up residence in Lviv. In May 1992 Ukrainian Catholic Bishops from all over the world convened for a synod in Lviv for the first time in many decades. And in August 1992 the remains of Cardinal Joseph Slipyj were translated from Rome to Lviv where he was buried next to Metropolitan Andrew Sheptyckyj. By late 1992 the church had over 2300 communities and churches, 11 bishops, over 1100 priests, 350 monks, about 800 nuns, and approximately 950 seminarians. The church's jurisdiction is currently limited to two dioceses in Galicia. But Ukrainian Catholic officials in Lviv believe that there are as many as six million faithful of their church scattered throughout Ukraine. Seminaries have been set up in Lviv and Ivano-Frankivsk.

Ukrainian Catholics also have a significant presence in Poland. When the Soviet Union annexed most of Galicia during World War II, about 1,300,000 Ukrainians remained in Poland. In 1946 the new Polish communist authorities deported most of these Ukrainians to the Soviet Union and suppressed the Ukrainian Catholic Church. Approximately 145,000 Ukrainian Catholics dispersed around the country were able to worship openly only in the Latin rite. Only in 1957 were pastoral centers opened to serve them. In 1989 Pope John Paul II appointed a Ukrainian bishop as auxiliary to the Polish Primate. He was named Bishop of Przemysl of the Ukrainians in January 1991, thus providing Ukrainian Catholics in Poland with their first diocesan bishop since the war. But in the general reshaping of the Polish ecclesiastical structures in 1992, it was made a suffragan of the Archdiocese of Warsaw and formally removed from the Metropolitan Province of Lviv to which it had belonged since 1818. In June 1993 the Przemysl diocese was made immediately subject to the Holy See.

There is a large diaspora of Ukrainian Catholics. In the United States there are four dioceses and 204 parishes for 145,000 members. The Metropolitan is Archbishop Stephen Sulyk of Philadelphia of the Ukrainians (827 North Franklin Street, Philadelphia, Pennsylvania 19123). In Canada there are five dioceses and 348 parishes with 193,000 faithful. The Metropolitan is Archbishop Michael Bzdel of Winnipeg of the Ukrainians (235 Scotia Street, Winnipeg, Manitoba R2V 1V7). The eight parishes serving an estimated 25,000 Ukrainian Catholics in Australia have been placed under the pastoral care of Most Rev. Peter Stasiuk, Bishop of Saints Peter and Paul of Melbourne (35 Canning Street, North Melbourne, Vic. 3051). There is an Apostolic Exarchate for Ukrainian Catholics in Great Britain, headed by Bishop Michael Kuchmiak (22 Binney Street, London W1Y 1YN), with 14 parishes and about 27,000 members.

In the diaspora there are major Ukrainian seminaries in Washington, DC, Ottawa, Canada, and Curitiba, Brazil. In addition, a Ukrainian College has existed in Rome since 1897.

Location: Ukraine, Poland, United States, Canada, Brazil,
Argentina, Australia, Western Europe
HEAD: Cardinal Myroslav Ivan Lubachivsky (born 1914, elected
1984, cardinal 1985)
Title: Major Archbishop of Lviv of the Ukrainians
Residence: Lviv, Ukraine
MEMBERSHIP: 4,889,000

## IV. D. 3. The Ruthenian Catholic Church

The motherland of the Ruthenian Catholic Church is now in
extreme western Ukraine southwest of the Carpathian mountains.
The area was known variously in the past as the Carpatho-Ukraine,
Carpatho-Ruthenia, Carpatho-Russia, Subcarpathia, and now as
Transcarpathia. Although the ecclesiastical term "Ruthenian" was
formerly used more broadly also to include Ukrainians, Belarusians
and Slovaks, it is now used by church authorities in a narrower sense
to denote this specific Byzantine Catholic Church. But in terms of
ethnicity, Ruthenian Catholics prefer to be called Rusyns. They are
closely related to the Ukrainians, and speak a dialect of the same
language. The traditional Rusyn homeland extends beyond
Transcarpathia into northeast Slovakia and the "Lemko" region of
extreme southeast Poland.

In the late 9th century, most of this area came under the control of
Catholic Hungary, which much later promoted Catholic missionary
work among its Orthodox population, including the Rusyns. This
activity culminated in the reception of 63 of their priests into the
Catholic Church on 24 April 1646 at the town of Užhorod. The Union
of Užhorod affected the Orthodox population of an area which
roughly corresponds to today's eastern Slovakia. In 1664 a union
took place at Mukačevo which involved the Orthodox in today's
Carpatho-Ukraine in the Soviet Union and the Hungarian diocese of
Hajdúdorog. A third union, which affected the Orthodox in the
county of Maramaros to the east of Mukačevo, took place in about

1713. Thus within 100 years after the 1664 Union of Užhorod, the Orthodox Church virtually ceased to exist in the region.

Early on there were jurisdictional conflicts over who would control the Ruthenian Catholic Church in this area. In spite of the desire of the Ruthenian Catholics to have their own ecclesiastical organization, for more than a century the Ruthenian bishop of Mukačevo was only the ritual vicar of the local Latin bishop, and Ruthenian priests served as assistants in Latin parishes. The dispute was resolved in 1771 by Pope Clement XIV who, at the request of Empress Maria-Theresa, erected the Ruthenian eparchy of Mukačevo and made it a suffragan of the Primate of Hungary. A seminary for Ruthenian Catholics was set up at Užhorod in 1778.

After World War I, Transcarpathia became part of the new republic of Czechoslovakia. There were two Byzantine Catholic dioceses at Mukačevo and Prešov. Although in the 1920's a group of these Ruthenian Catholics returned to the Orthodox Church [see Orthodox Church in the Czech and Slovak Republics: III.A.14], Rusyn ethnic identity remained closely tied to the Ruthenian Catholic Church.

At the end of World War II, Transcarpathia, including Užhorod and Mukačevo, was annexed to the Soviet Union as part of the Ukrainian Soviet Socialist Republic. Prešov, however, remained in Czechoslovakia [see Slovak Catholic Church: IV.D.8]. The Soviet authorities soon initiated a vicious persecution of the Ruthenian Church in the newly acquired region. In 1946 the Užhorod seminary was closed, and in 1949 the Ruthenian Catholic Church was integrated into the Russian Orthodox Church. Rusyns on the other side of the Czechoslovak border were also forced to become Orthodox, while those in the Polish Lemko region were deported *en masse* in 1947 either to the Soviet Union or other parts of Poland. In all three countries, an attempt was made to wipe out any residual Rusyn national identity by declaring them all to be Orthodox and Ukrainian.

The collapse of communism throughout the region had a dramatic effect on Ruthenian Catholics. The first changes took place in Poland in the mid-1980's, where Lemko organizations began to surface and press for recognition of their rights and distinct status. In

Czechoslovakia, the much-diminished Ruthenian Catholic minority began in November 1989 to press for recognition within the predominantly Slovak Greek Catholic diocese of Prešov. And finally, in the Transcarpathian heartland, the Ruthenian Catholic eparchy of Mukačevo was reestablished when the Holy See appointed a bishop and two auxiliaries in January 1991. Many former churches were regained and a new seminary was being build in Užhorod.

A continuing issue for Ruthenian Catholics will be their relationship with the much larger Ukrainian Catholic Church. For the first time ever, the Mukačevo diocese finds itself functioning freely in the same country with the Ukrainian Catholic Church. Although it is not officially a part of the Ukrainian church, and is still immediately subject to the Holy See, Ruthenian Catholic bishops have attended recent Ukrainian Catholic synods. The bishop of Mukačevo has made it clear, however, that he opposes integration into the Ukrainian Catholic Church, and favors the promotion of the distinct national and religious identity of his Rusyn people.

Many Ruthenian Catholics had immigrated to North America in the late 19th and early 20th centuries. Because of strained relations with the local Latin hierarchy, and the lack of recognition of such legitimate Ruthenian Catholic traditions as a married clergy, large numbers of these Catholics returned to the Orthodox Church. In 1982 it was estimated that out of 690,000 people of Rusyn descent in the United States, 225,000 were still Ruthenian Catholics, 95,000 belonged to the Carpatho-Russian Orthodox diocese [see III.C.1], 250,000 were in the Orthodox Church in America [see III.A.15], 20,000 were in Orthodox parishes directly under the Moscow Patriarchate, and 100,000 belonged to various other Orthodox, Ukrainian Catholic, Roman Catholic, and Protestant denominations.

In many areas of the diaspora, including Australia, Great Britain, and Canada, Ruthenian Catholics are not distinguished from Ukrainian Catholics. In the United States, however, they have a separate ecclesiastical structure with four dioceses, 251 parishes, and about 211,000 members. The Metropolitan Diocese of Pittsburg fell vacant in April 1993 with the death of Archbishop Thomas Dolinay (54 Riverview Avenue, Pittsburgh, Pennsylvania 15214). This church, generally known simply as "Byzantine Catholic," emphasizes its American character, and celebrates liturgy in English in most parishes. Candidates for the priesthood are trained at Sts. Cyril and Methodius Seminary in Pittsburgh.

Although Bishop Semedi of the mother diocese of Mukačevo is listed here as "head" of the Ruthenian Catholic Church, the Metropolitan Province in the United States is not dependent on him.

LOCATION: Ukraine, United States

HEAD: Bishop Ivan Semedi

Title: Bishop of Mukačevo of the Byzantines

Residence: Užhorod, Ukraine

MEMBERSHIP: 511,000

## IV. D. 4. The Romanian Catholic Church

Transylvania, presently one of the three major regions of Romania along with Wallachia and Moldavia, became part of Hungary in the early 11th century. Although the principality was also home to large numbers of Hungarians and Germans, who were mostly Latin Catholics, Orthodox Romanians made up the majority of the population. Soon after the province was taken by the Turks in the 16th century, Calvinism became widespread among the Hungarians, and Lutheranism among the Germans.

In 1687, the Hapsburg Austrian emperor Leopold I drove the Turks from Transylvania and annexed it to his empire. It was his policy to encourage Orthodox within his realm to become Byzantine Catholics. For this purpose the Jesuits began to work as missionaries among the Transylvanian Romanians in 1693. Their efforts, combined with the denial of full civil rights to the Orthodox, and the spread of Protestantism in the area which caused growing concern among the Orthodox clergy, all contributed to the acceptance of a union with Rome by Orthodox Metropolitan Atanasie of Transylvania in 1698. He later convoked a synod which formally concluded the agreement on 4 September 1700.

At first this union included most of the Romanian Orthodox in the province. But in 1744, the Orthodox monk Visarion led a popular uprising which sparked a widespread movement back towards Orthodoxy. In spite of government efforts to enforce the union with Rome — even by military means — resistance was such that Empress Maria Theresa reluctantly allowed the appointment of a bishop for the Romanian Orthodox in Transylvania in 1759. In the end, about half of the Transylvanian Romanians returned to Orthodoxy.

It proved difficult for the new Byzantine Catholic community, known popularly as the "Greek Catholic Church," to obtain in practice the religious and civil rights that had been guaranteed it when the union was consummated. Bishop Ion Inochentie Micu-Klein, head of the church from 1729 to 1751, struggled with great vigor for the rights of his church and of all Romanians within the empire.

The Romanian Greek Catholic dioceses had originally been subordinate to the Latin Hungarian Primate at Esztergom. But in 1853 Pope Pius IX established a separate metropolitan province for the Greek Catholics in Transylvania. The diocese of Făgăraş-Alba Julia was made metropolitan see, with three suffragan dioceses. Since 1737 the bishops of Făgăraş had resided at Blaj, which had become the church's administrative and cultural center. Romanian Greek Catholic synods were held at Blaj in 1872, 1882, and 1900 which drafted legislation governing the life of the church.

At the end of World War I, Transylvania was united to Romania, and for the first time Greek Catholics found themselves in a predominantly Orthodox state. By 1940 there were five dioceses, over 1,500 priests (90% of whom were married), and about 1½ million faithful. Major seminaries existed at Blaj, Oradea Mare, and Gherla. A Pontifical Romanian College in Rome received its first students in 1936.

But the establishment of a communist government in Romania after World War II proved disastrous for the Romanian Greek Catholic Church. On October 1, 1948, 36 Greek Catholic priests met under government pressure at Cluj-Napoca. They voted to terminate the union with Rome and asked for reunion with the Romanian

Orthodox Church. On October 21 it was formally abolished at a ceremony at Alba Julia. On December 1, 1948, the government passed legislation which dissolved the Greek Catholic Church and gave over most of its property to the Orthodox Church. The six Greek Catholic bishops were arrested on the night of December 29-30. Five of the six later died in prison. In 1964 the bishop of Cluj-Gherla, Juliu Hossu, was released from prison but placed under house arrest in a monastery, where he died in 1970. Pope Paul VI announced in 1973 that he had made Hossu a Cardinal *in pectore* in 1969.

After 41 years underground, the fortunes of the Greek Catholic Church in Romania changed dramatically after the Ceauşescu regime was overthrown in December 1989. On 2 January 1990 the 1948 decree which dissolved the church was abrogated. Greek Catholics began to worship openly again, and three secretly-ordained bishops emerged from hiding. In March 1990, Pope John Paul II reestablished the hierarchy of the church by appointing bishops for all five dioceses.

Unfortunately the reemergence of the Greek Catholic Church has been accompanied by a confrontation with the Romanian Orthodox Church over the restitution of church buildings. The Catholics insisted that all property be returned as a matter of justice, while the Orthodox held that any transfer of property must take into account the present pastoral needs of both communities. As of March 1993 this impasse had not been overcome, and only 66 churches had been returned to the Greek Catholics. But seminaries had begun functioning at Cluj, Baia Mare, and Oradea, and theological institutes had been set up in Blaj, Cluj and Oradea. In Romania this church calls itself "The Romanian Church United with Rome."

The size of the Romanian Greek Catholic Church is hotly disputed. They themselves officially claim just under two million (reflected in the figure given below) and in some publications state that they may be as many as three million. But a Romanian census carried out in January 1992 reported only 228,377 members, a figure the Greek Catholics rejected.

There is a small diaspora of Romanian Greek Catholics. The only diocese is St. George's in Canton of the Romanians which includes all the faithful in the United States. It is presided over by Bishop Vasile Louis Puscas (1121 44th Street NE, Canton, Ohio 44714), and has 15 parishes for about 5,200 faithful.

LOCATION: Romania, USA, Canada
HEAD: Cardinal Alexandru Todea (born 1913, appointed 1990)
Title: Archbishop of Făgăraş and Alba Julia
Residence: Blaj, Romania
MEMBERSHIP: 1,848,000


## IV. D. 5. The Greek Catholic Church

The Ottoman Sultan Mohammed II removed his non-Latin Catholic subjects from the civil authority of the Patriarch of Constantinople in 1829. The formation of Byzantine Catholic communities in the empire was now possible for the first time.

A Latin priest, Fr. John Marangos, began missionary work among the Greek Orthodox in Constantinople in 1856 and eventually formed a very small group of Byzantine Catholics. He died in 1878, and was succeeded by Fr. Polycarp Anastasiadis, a former student at the Orthodox Theological School at Halki. In the 1880's Byzantine Catholic communities were also formed in two villages in Thrace.

In 1895 the French Assumptionist Fathers began work in Constantinople where they founded a seminary and two small Greek Byzantine Catholic parishes. These Assumptionists were distinguished above all for the valuable scholarly studies they produced on the Eastern Churches.

In 1911 Pope Pius X created an Apostolic Exarchate for the Byzantine rite Catholics in Turkey and named Fr. Isaias Papadopoulos as its first bishop. He was succeeded in 1920 by Bishop George Calavassy (died 1957). It was his task to oversee the immigration of virtually the entire Byzantine Catholic community of Constantinople to Athens, and those of the two villages in Thrace to a town in Macedonia. This was part of a general exchange of populations that took place between Greece and Turkey in the 1920's. In view of this new situation, the Holy See erected a separate Apostolic Exarchate in Athens for Byzantine Catholics in Greece in 1923.

Although their presence in Greece aroused the anger of the local Orthodox hierarchy, these Greek Catholics were determined to serve their fellow countrymen by works of charity and social assistance. In 1944 they founded the Pammakaristos hospital in Athens, which became known as one of the best in the nation.

The Greek Orthodox Church remains very hostile to the very idea of the existence of this church, which it views as a gratuitous creation of the Catholic Church in Orthodox territory. It is still illegal in Greece for Catholic priests to dress in a way typical of Orthodox clergy. In 1975 a new bishop was appointed for the Byzantine Catholics in Greece over the strong objections of the Orthodox Archbishop of Athens.

The community remains very small. In Greece, most of the faithful live in Athens, while in Turkey one small parish exists in Istanbul. There are currently 12 priests serving the church, all of them celibate and originally of the Latin rite.

LOCATION: Greece and Turkey
HEAD: Bishop Anarghyros Printesis (born 1937, appointed 1975)
Title: Apostolic Exarch for Greek Catholics of the Byzantine rite
Residence: Athens, Greece
MEMBERSHIP: 2,350

## IV. D. 6. Byzantine Catholics in former Yugoslavia

The first Byzantine Catholics in what would later be Yugoslavia were Serbians living in Hungarian-controlled Croatia in the early 17th century. In 1611 they were given a bishop who served as Byzantine vicar of the Latin Bishop of Zagreb. He had his headquarters at Marcha monastery, which became a center of efforts to bring Serbian Orthodox faithful in Croatia into communion with Rome.

After a period of tension with the local Latin bishops, the Serbs in Croatia were given their own diocesan bishop by Pope Pius VI on 17

June 1777, with his see at Križevci, near Zagreb. At first he was made suffragan to the primate of Hungary, and later (1853) to the Latin Archbishop of Zagreb.

The diocese of Križevci was extended to embrace all the Byzantine Catholics in Yugoslavia when the country was founded after World War I. The diocese included five distinct groups: some ethnic Serbs in Croatia, Ruthenians who had emigrated from Slovakia around 1750, Ukrainians who emigrated from Galicia in about 1900, Slavic Macedonians in the south of the country who became Catholic through missionary activity in the 19th century (they now have their own Apostolic Visitator), and a few Romanians in the Yugoslavian Banat.

The diocese of Križevci still includes all the Byzantine Catholics in the former republics of Yugoslavia. It remains to be seen whether this arrangement will continue after the break-up of the country into several independent nations.

LOCATION: The republics of former Yugoslavia
HEAD: Bishop Slavomir Miklovš (born 1934, appointed 1983)
Title: Bishop of Križevci
Residence: Zagreb, Croatia
MEMBERSHIP: 49,000

## IV. D. 7. The Bulgarian Catholic Church

Under Ottoman rule, Bulgarian Orthodox Christians [see III.A.8], who twice before had had their own Patriarchate, were gradually brought under the control of ethnic Greek bishops as part of a general hellenization of their ecclesial life. In 1767 they were placed directly under the jurisdiction of the Greek Patriarch of Constantinople.

In the 19th century, when a struggle to obtain ecclesiastical independence from the Ecumenical Patriarchate was gaining momentum, some influential Bulgarian Orthodox in Constantinople began to consider union with Rome as a solution to their problem. They thought that as Catholics they would be able to retrieve their national ecclesiastical traditions which they felt Constantinople had denied them.

In 1861 they sent a delegation, headed by the elderly Archimandrite Joseph Sokolsky, to Rome to negotiate with the Holy See. These talks were successful: Pope Pius IX himself ordained Sokolsky a bishop on 8 April 1861 and named him Archbishop for Bulgarian Catholics of the Byzantine rite. The following June he was recognized as such by the Ottoman government.

But in June 1861, almost immediately after his return to Constantinople, Sokolsky disappeared under very mysterious circumstances, was taken to Odessa on a Russian ship, and spent the remaining 18 years of his life in the Monastery of the Caves at Kiev. It has never been established whether he returned to Orthodoxy and fled, or was abducted.

Nevertheless, having successfully identified itself with the Bulgarian nationalist movement, the Bulgarian Byzantine Catholic Church initially gained about 60,000 members. The Russian government, meanwhile, began to support attempts to establish a separate Bulgarian Orthodox Church within the Ottoman Empire. This effort bore fruit in 1870 when a distinct Bulgarian Orthodox Exarchate was set up. This effectively put an end to the movement towards Catholicism, and before the turn of the century, three quarters of the Bulgarian Byzantine Catholics had returned to Orthodoxy.

Most of those who remained Byzantine Catholic lived in villages in Macedonia and Thrace. Therefore in 1883 the Holy See created a new ecclesiastical organization for them. Apostolic Vicariates were established in Thessalonika for Macedonia and in Adrianople for Thrace, while an Apostolic Administrator with the title of Archbishop remained in Constantinople. But the community suffered grievously during the Balkan Wars of 1912-1913, and the few surviving members fled to the new Bulgarian kingdom for safety.

Given this new situation, Bulgarian Byzantine Catholics were reorganized in 1926: the previous ecclesiastical entities were abolished, and a new Apostolic Exarchate was established in Sofia. This was accomplished on the advice of the Apostolic Visitator (1925-1931) and later Apostolic Delegate (1931-1934) to Bulgaria, Archbishop Angelo Roncalli, subsequently Pope John XXIII. He also supported the opening of an interritual seminary in Sofia in 1934 which was directed by the Jesuits until it was closed in 1945.

Unlike most other Byzantine Catholic Churches in Eastern Europe, this church was allowed to function openly during the communist regime in Bulgaria, although with many restrictions. The end of communism has brought new freedom and growth.

LOCATION: Bulgaria

HEAD: Bishop Metodi Dimitrov Stratiev (born 1916, appointed 1971)

Title: Apostolic Exarch for Catholics of the Byzantine-Slav rite in Bulgaria

Residence: Sofia, Bulgaria

MEMBERSHIP: 25,000


## IV. D. 8. The Slovak Catholic Church

The religious history of Byzantine Catholics in Slovakia is closely related to that of the Ruthenians [see IV.D.3]. Indeed, for centuries their histories were intertwined, since the 1646 Union of Užhorod was virtually unanimously accepted in the territory which is now eastern Slovakia.

At the end of World War I, most Byzantine Catholic Ruthenians and Slovaks were included within the territory of the new Czechoslovak republic. During the interwar period a significant movement towards Orthodoxy took place within this church. In 1937 the Byzantine diocese of Prešov was removed from the jurisdiction of the Hungarian primate and made immediately subject to the Holy See.

At the end of World War II, Transcarpathia was annexed by the Soviet Union. The diocese of Prešov then included all Byzantine Catholics in Czechoslovakia.

In April 1950, soon after the communist take-over of Czechoslovakia, a "synod" was convoked at Prešov at which five priests and a number of laymen signed a document declaring that the union with Rome was dissolved and asking to be received into the jurisdiction of the Moscow Patriarchate (later the Orthodox Church of Czechoslovakia). Greek Catholic Bishop Gojdic of Prešov and his auxiliary were imprisoned. Bishop Gojdic died in prison in 1960.

This situation persisted until 1968 when, under the influence of the "Prague Spring" presided over by Alexander Dubcek, former Byzantine Catholic parishes were allowed to return to Catholicism if they so desired. Of 292 parishes involved, 205 voted to return to communion with Rome. This was one of the few Dubcek reforms which survived the Soviet invasion of 1968. Most of their church buildings, however, remained in the hands of the Orthodox. But under the new non-communist independent Slovak government, most of these had been returned to the Slovak Byzantine Catholic Church by 1993.

The Prešov diocese has long included a significant number of Byzantine Catholics who are ethnic Rusyns [see Ruthenian Catholic Church, IV.D.3] as well as Slovaks. In recent times, however, they have to a certain extent been absorbed into Slovak culture, as very few religious books are available in Rusyn, and the liturgy is almost always celebrated in either Church Slavonic or Slovak.

There is a small diaspora of the faithful of this church. In the United States and most other areas, they are not distinguished from the Ruthenians. They have a separate diocese, however, in Canada, presided over by Bishop Michael Rusnak (Diocese of Sts. Cyril and Methodius of Toronto, PO Box 70, 223 Carlton Road, Unionville, Ontario L3R 2L8). There are 28 parishes for about 30,000 Slovak Catholics.

LOCATION: Slovakia, Czech Republic, Canada
HEAD: Bishop Ján Hirka (born 1923, appointed 1989)
Title: Bishop of Prešov of Catholics of the Byzantine Rite
Residence: Prešov, Slovakia
MEMBERSHIP: 430,000

## IV. D. 9. The Hungarian Catholic Church

Most of the members of this church are not ethnic Hungarians, but are descended from the many Byzantine Christians of other nationalities who settled in Hungary over the centuries and eventually became Hungarian-speaking. Nevertheless, many maintain that there is at least a partial link between this community and the significant Byzantine church that existed in Hungary in the Middle Ages. Indeed, there were several Byzantine monasteries in Hungary in the 11th and 12th centuries, but all of them were destroyed during the 13th-century Tatar invasions.

It was in the 15th and 16th centuries, due to widespread population shifts caused by the Turkish invasions, that communities of Byzantine Serbs, Ruthenians, Slovaks and Greeks moved into the area. Most of them eventually became Catholic but retained their Byzantine heritage. In the 18th century a number of Hungarian Protestants became Catholic and chose the Byzantine rite, again adding to the number of Byzantine Catholics in Hungary. They were placed under the jurisdiction of non-Hungarian Byzantine bishops.

Because a significant community of Byzantine Catholics otherwise entirely integrated into Hungarian society now existed, some began to press for the use of the Hungarian language in the liturgy. But such a proposal was resisted by the church authorities. For this reason, the first Hungarian translation of the liturgy of John Chrysostom had to be published privately in 1795. Through the 19th century several other liturgical books were published in Hungarian, still without the approval of the ecclesiastical authorities.

In 1900 a large group of Hungarian Byzantine Catholic pilgrims presented Pope Leo XIII with a petition requesting that a separate Byzantine diocese be established in the country, with the right to use Hungarian in the liturgy. Finally, in 1912 Pope Pius X erected the diocese of Hajdúdorog for Hungarian Byzantine Catholics. But he made Greek the obligatory liturgical language, and gave priests three years to learn it. World War I intervened, however, and the requirement to use Greek was never enforced. The use of Hungarian gained ground and, willy-nilly, by the 1930's, all the main liturgical texts had been translated.

In 1923 an apostolic exarchate was established at Miskolc for 21 Ruthenian parishes formerly in the diocese of Prešov that remained in Hungarian territory after Czechoslovakia was created. They were provided with a distinct identity because they used Slavonic in the liturgy. By the 1940's, however, they had all begun to use Hungarian, and the apostolic exarchate since that time has been administered by the bishop of Hajdúdorog.

The diocese of Hajdúdorog originally covered only areas of the country in which Byzantine Catholics were concentrated. But in 1968 its jurisdiction was extended to all Byzantine rite Catholics in Hungary. There is a seminary at Nyiregyháza.

The rather small number of Eastern rite Hungarians who immigrated to North America have a few parishes, all of them part of the Ruthenian dioceses in the USA and the Ukrainian dioceses in Canada.

LOCATION: Hungary
HEAD: Bishop Szilárd Keresztes (born 1932, appointed 1988)
Title: Bishop of Hajdúdorog, Apostolic Administrator of Miskolc
Residence: Nyiregyháza, Hungary
MEMBERSHIP: 280,000

## IV. D. 10. Eastern Catholic Communities Without Hierarchies

**Russians**: From the early 19th century until 1905, Byzantine Catholicism was illegal in the Russian Empire. But after Czar Nicholas II issued his edict of religious toleration, a few small communities of Byzantine Catholics were formed. In 1917 an Apostolic Exarchate was established for them. But this was soon followed by the communist revolution, after which the group was virtually annihilated. A second Apostolic Exarchate was set up for the few Russian Byzantine Catholics in China in 1928 based in Harbin [see Orthodox Church of China: III.B.4]. This was always an extremely small community, and today approximately 3,500 live in the diaspora. A Russian College, the "Russicum" was founded in Rome in 1929 under Jesuit supervision to train clergy to work with Russian emigrés and in Russia itself. The Apostolic Exarchates in Russia and China are still officially extant, but as of mid-1993 had not been reconstituted. There are four Russian Byzantine Catholic parishes in the United States, and one in Melbourne, Australia.

**Belarusians**: Like their Ukrainian counterparts [see IV.D.2], Belarusian Catholics originated in the Union of Brest (1595-1596). But the Belarusian Byzantine Catholic Church was suppressed by the Russian imperial government along with the Ukrainian Catholic Church in the 19th century.

After World War I, a community of about 30,000 Byzantine Catholics emerged in areas of Belarus which were now part of Poland. An Apostolic Visitator was appointed for them in 1931, and an Exarch in 1940. But after World War II, when the area was absorbed by the Soviet Union, the church was again suppressed and integrated into the Russian Orthodox Church.

Following the collapse of communism and the independence of Belarus in 1991, Belarusian Byzantine Catholics began to emerge once again. A survey of religious affiliation undertaken by the Belarus State University in 1992 indicated that about 100,000 Belarusians identified themselves as Byzantine Catholic. And by June 1993, there were 16 Belarusian Byzantine Catholic parishes in the country where, unlike in the Roman Catholic and Orthodox ones, the liturgy was being celebrated in the Belarusian language.

There are about 5,000 Belarusian Byzantine Catholics in the diaspora. They have a parish in Chicago, Illinois, USA, and a Religious and Cultural Centre in London, England.

**Georgians**: Catholic missionaries began to work in the Georgian kingdom in the 13th century, setting up small Latin communities. A Latin diocese existed in Tbilisi from 1329 to 1507. In 1626 missionaries began to work specifically with Georgian Orthodox faithful [see III.A.9]. In 1845, the Russian government, which had controlled Georgia since 1801, expelled the Catholic missionaries. But in 1848 Czar Nicholas I agreed to the creation of a Latin diocese at Tiraspol with jurisdiction over Catholics in the vast southern regions of the empire, including Georgia.

A small community of Armenian Catholics existed in Georgia since the 18th century. Because the czars forbade Catholics to use the Byzantine rite, and the Holy See did not promote its use among the Georgians, no organized Georgian Byzantine Catholic Church ever existed. In 1920 it was estimated that of 40,000 Catholics in Georgia, 32,000 were Latins and the remainder of the Armenian rite. However, a small Georgian Byzantine Catholic parish has long existed in Istanbul. Currently it is without a priest. Twin male and female religious orders "of the Immaculate Conception" were founded there in 1861, but have since died out.

After Georgia became independent again in 1991, the Catholic Church was able to function more freely, and a significant Armenian Catholic community was able to resume a normal ecclesial life.

**Albanians**: The first community of Byzantine Catholic Albanians was a small mission along the coast of Epirus which existed from 1628 to 1765. A second group was established in about 1900 by a former Albanian Orthodox priest, Fr. George Germanos. By 1912 his community numbered about 120, and was centered in the village of Elbasan. In 1938 monks from the Italo-Albanian monastery at Grottaferrata came to assist the community which by 1945 had about 400 members. The group vanished after 1967 when Albania was declared an atheist state. There is no indication that it has been reestablished after the fall of communism, although an Apostolic Administration for Byzantine Catholics in Southern Albania still exists, headed since December 1992 by the Apostolic Pro-Nuncio in Tirana.

# Appendix I

## *Catholic-Orthodox Relations in Post-Communist Europe: Ghosts from the Past and Challenges for the Future*

In December 1991, Pope John Paul II convened a special Synod of Bishops of Europe. Although fraternal delegates from other churches and ecclesial communities were invited to participate, the Orthodox Churches were almost completely absent. To explain why this was so, the Ecumenical Patriarchate sent Metropolitan Spyridon of Italy to the Synod.

In his speech in the presence of the Pope, the Metropolitan said that the Orthodox absence was due to the tensions that existed between Catholics and Orthodox in Eastern and Central Europe. He listed two main reasons for this: first, that the rebirth of so-called "uniate" churches in that region had been accompanied by acts of violence, and, secondly, that the setting up of parallel Catholic ecclesiastical structures in those countries exceeded what was required to care for the local Catholic populations. The Metropolitan continued:

> The impression is now widespread among the Orthodox that [the Catholic Church] is distancing itself from the Second Vatican Council, and that the territories of countries which have been Orthodox for centuries, now liberated from the communist regimes, are being considered by their Roman Catholic brothers as «terra missionis».[1]

The bishop warned that the situation was so bad that the theological dialogue might be suspended, or even completely broken off.

Similar concerns had been expressed by the Holy Synod of the Moscow Patriarchate the previous October when it responded

---

[1] "Prospettive della Chiesa Ortodossa," *L'Osservatore Romano*, 4 December 1991, page 4.

negatively to the papal invitation.[2] And two months later, in February 1992, the Holy Synod of the Church of Greece issued a strongly-worded statement charging Pope John Paul II with being deceitful and dishonest in his relations with the Orthodox. The Greek Bishops also accused the Holy See of using the Byzantine Catholic Churches to extend its influence in Orthodox countries and called upon the Greek government to break off diplomatic relations with the Vatican.[3]

It is quite clear, then, that Catholic-Orthodox relations are going through a difficult period. The fall of communism in Eastern and Central Europe, while obviously a good thing, has caused old problems to resurface, and has created serious difficulties for the international commission for dialogue between the two churches.

To gain a better understanding of these problems, I would like this evening to look back into the history of Catholic-Orthodox relations, with special emphasis on the origins of the policy of uniatism and the formation of the Byzantine Catholic Churches, and the Orthodox reaction to this policy. I will then try to show the way in which this history affects the present situation, and examine the approach the international commission has taken to the problem. And finally, I will try to identify some of the challenges that the Catholic and Orthodox Churches face in view of their contemporary ecumenical relationship.

## I. Historical Background

The year 1054 has traditionally been identified as the date of the schism between East and West. But more recent scholarship has tended to view the separation between Latins and Byzantines more as what Yves Congar has described as a "mutual estrangement" — a gradual isolation and loss of the ability to understand one another. The excommunications of 1054 were a high point in that process, but certainly ordinary Italians or Greeks were initially unaffected by it. It

---

[2] Italian text in *Adista* news service, 21-23 October 1991, pp. 3-4.

[3] Dimitri Salachas, "Il papa: né sincero né fraterno," *Il regno-attualità*, June 1992, pp. 132-135.

was only much later, in the wake of the Crusades, which saw the sacking of Constantinople by the Latin Crusaders in 1204, and the replacement of the Greek hierarchy by a Latin one in the Holy Land, that the rift progressively became embedded in the collective consciousness of both communions.

In 1274 at the Second Council of Lyons and in 1439 at the Council of Ferrara-Florence, Bishops and theologians of the two churches thrashed out their differences and eventually agreed on a formula for reunion. But the conciliar agreements were not accepted in the East, and the two churches lapsed into a period of almost total isolation from one another — and a *de facto* refusal to even recognize each other as churches — which would endure for centuries.

This new situation, in which it was perceived that dialogue between the hierarchies of the two churches had proven useless, set the scene for the development of a new Catholic policy towards the Orthodox East. What this policy would be was greatly affected by other developments within the Latin Church at that time, such as the fragmentation of the West and the emergence of the nation states, and especially the shock of the Protestant Reformation. The Council of Trent was called to consider the need for new ecclesial structures and reform. A strong centralizing tendency ensued, which vigorously emphasized uniformity and obedience to the authority of the papacy as essential for authentic ecclesial life.[4] Within this context, it became possible to speak of reconciliation with the Orthodox only as a "return" to Roman obedience. And it provided a theological justification for the sending of Catholic missionaries to work among the "dissidents" for the purpose of bringing them back to Catholic unity. A corollary to this policy was the simultaneous development of the notion of "rite." The emphasis on unity remained. But it now became possible for groups of separated Eastern Christians who came into union with Rome to be absorbed into the single Church, while being allowed to maintain their own liturgical tradition and elements of

---

[4] Emmanuel Lanne, "The Connection between the Post-Tridentine Concept of Primacy and the Emerging of the Uniate Churches," *Wort und Wahrheit* Supplementary Issue Number 4 (December 1978) 99-108.

their own canonical discipline.[5] It is this new policy towards the Orthodox East that is now called uniatism.

So this was the dominant outlook when significant concrete unions with sections of some Orthodox Churches began to take place. And the initial results were impressive. In 1595 the Union of Brest achieved union with the entire Orthodox Metropolitan Province of Kiev. This covered a vast area that is now the western half of Ukraine and Belarus. In 1646 the Union of Užhorod was the first of a series of reconciliations with Orthodox dioceses which would eventually include all of the Ruthenians under Hungarian rule. In 1700 there was a Union with most of the Romanian Orthodox in Transylvania, then a Hungarian province. And in 1724 there was a schism in the Greek Patriarchate of Antioch between pro- and anti-Catholic parties which led to the formation of the Melkite Catholic Church.[6]

By the early 19th century, the situation had stabilized somewhat. The vast majority of Catholic and Orthodox Byzantine Christians in the world lived within one of three great empires: the Russian, Austro-Hungarian, and Ottoman. The Russian Orthodox czars vigorously opposed Eastern Catholicism and suppressed it within their domain. Thus most of what is now Ukraine and Belarus had become Orthodox once again when the Russians conquered the area. In the Ottoman Empire, Catholic missionaries had sometimes been free to pursue their mission among the Orthodox largely because of pressure applied by the French government on the sultans. But at other times the Eastern Catholics had been severely persecuted. The

---

[5] Yves Congar, *Diversity and Communion*. English translation by John Bowden. (London: SCM Press, 1984) 81-82.

[6] On the Union of Brest see J. Macha, *Ecclesiastical Unification: A Theoretical Framework Together with Case Studies from the History of Latin-Byzantine Relations*, Orientalia Christiana Analecta 198 (Rome: Pontifical Oriental Institute, 1974. On the union of the Romanians in Transylvania: K. Hitchins, "Religion and Rumanian National Consciousness in Eighteenth-Century Transylvania," *The Slavonic and East European Review* 57 (1979) 214-239. On the Melkites see S. Descy, *Introduction à l'histoire et l'ecclésiologie de l'Église melkite* (Beirut: Editions Saint Paul, 1986).

great majority of Byzantine Catholics lived in the Austro-Hungarian Empire. The Austrians had actively promoted the formation of Byzantine Catholic Churches, so that relatively few Orthodox remained within the Hapsburg realm.

It is very dangerous to generalize about the histories of these unions. And it should be emphasized that some of them corresponded to spontaneous pro-Catholic movements among the Orthodox, as was the case, for example, in the Union of Brest and the much smaller Bulgarian Byzantine Catholic Church.[7] And the Maronites in Lebanon claim to have never broken communion with the see of Rome.

By and large, however, these unions can be grouped into three basic categories. By far the most successful model was the one employed within the Austro-Hungarian Empire. Here whole Orthodox dioceses or ecclesiastical provinces were received into the Catholic Church. Such was the case in the Unions of Alba Iulia with the Romanians, and Užhorod with what are now called the Ruthenians. In this model, the efforts of Catholic missionaries were supported by a Catholic government which denied certain civil rights to its Orthodox subjects in order to encourage them to become Byzantine Catholic.

According to the second model, more typical of the Middle East, Catholic missionaries would work to create a sizeable pro-Catholic party within a local Orthodox Church, and then try to secure the election of Bishops and even a Patriarch with these views. The Catholics hoped to achieve union with entire Orthodox Churches in this way, but they did not anticipate how strong the Orthodox reaction would be. In these cases, the Orthodox party then elected its own Patriarch, thus establishing a parallel hierarchy and splitting the church. This is what happened in the Greek Patriarchate of Antioch

---

[7] On the Bulgarian Byzantine Catholic Church, see C. Walter, "Raphael Popov, Bulgarian Uniate Bishop: Problems of Uniatism and Autocephaly," *Sobornost Incorporating Eastern Churches Review* 6 (1984) 46-60.

in 1724, and earlier in the non-Chalcedonian Syrian Orthodox Church.[8]

The third model called for Catholic missionaries to work outside the Orthodox Churches, setting up Byzantine Catholic counterparts to draw Orthodox faithful away from them. The hope was that by a gradual process of attrition, the Orthodox Churches would be entirely replaced by Byzantine Catholic ones. In the end this method was not very successful, and led only to the creation of very small Byzantine Catholic communities, and yet it evoked the strongest Orthodox reaction.

We can gain an insight into Orthodox feelings on this matter by examining the connection Catholic missionaries saw between their work among the Orthodox and the adoption of the Byzantine rite. A French Assumptionist patrologist, Fulbert Cayré (1884-1971) shed some light on this matter at a conference he gave at Louvain University in 1923 on "The Methods of the Oriental Apostolate."[9] Cayré was living in Constantinople where his community had set up a Byzantine-rite mission to work among the Greek Orthodox of the city.

Cayré's fundamental thesis, like the third model mentioned above, was that the promotion of Byzantine Catholicism is by far the most effective method of bringing dissident Orthodox back to Catholic unity. The efforts of Latin missionaries had born little fruit, but the conversion of large numbers of Orthodox to Catholicism could still be achieved through the method of opposing Byzantine Catholic Churches to the local Orthodox ones. When they see a church of their own rite obedient to the Pope, but which nevertheless scrupulously maintains all its Orthodox usages, Cayré affirmed, they will realize that they have nothing to loose in breaking with the schism:

---

[8] Wilhelm de Vries, *Ortodossia e cattolicesimo*, Trans. from German by Enzo Gatti, (Brescia: Queriniana, 1983) 118.

[9] Fulbert Cayré, "Les méthodes d'apostolat oriental," *L'Union des Églises* 2 (1923) 195-198, 228-230, 260-261.

Here are those who can most effectively work for the Union in the East, those who can directly address the dissidents to propose that they enter into the Roman communion, those who can obtain not just a few rare individual returns [to Catholic unity], perhaps scattered over several years, as one finds in centers where Latin missionaries are working, but who can bring about numerous returns, and even bring about the return of several important groups at the same time. It is in this way, and this way only, that one can foresee . . . the end of the schism. The whole question of the union, therefore, boils down to the formation of an instructed, pious and zealous Eastern Catholic clergy.[10]

Cayré went on to describe the indirect role that Latin missionaries could play in those regions by undertaking works of charity, especially by setting up Catholic schools for Orthodox students, which would be like "nurseries" for new Catholics.

I do not mean to present this outlook as the only one which existed in the Catholic Church at the time. Already the seeds of a new attitude were being planted by such Catholic churchmen as Dom Lambert Beaudoin, the founder of the Benedictine monastery now at Chevetogne.[11] Nevertheless, the way of thinking Cayré presented at Louvain was predominant, and enjoyed official support. And it goes a long way towards explaining the very strong Orthodox reaction to the policy of uniatism, especially among the Greeks.

And the reaction was very strong indeed. In fact, there is some evidence that the official denial of the validity of Catholic baptism by some Orthodox churches can be seen as pastoral responses to the threat they saw in uniatism. The Union of Brest took place in 1595, and in 1620 the Holy Synod of the Russian Orthodox Church decreed that Catholics should be rebaptized. The Melkite schism in the Greek Orthodox Patriarchate of Antioch took place in 1724, and in 1755 Patriarch Cyril V of Constantinople issued an encyclical requiring

---

[10] Ibid., p. 198.

[11] On this see Etienne Fouilloux, "Dom Lambert entre l'unionisme et l'oecuménisme, *Unité des chrétiens* 29 (January 1978) 11-13.

the same.[12] By denying the validity of Catholic baptism, the Orthodox hierarchy hoped to counter the Byzantine Catholic claim that for Orthodox to enter into communion with Rome was a small matter entailing only minimal changes in their traditional ecclesial life.

In addition, there has always been a strong Orthodox feeling that Byzantine Catholic clergy are deceptive, that they attempt to win over converts among the uneducated by posing as Orthodox priests. This was the position taken in the 1920's by the Orthodox Archbishop Chrysostomos of Athens in his correspondence with George Calavassy, the Byzantine Catholic bishop in the same city. The Orthodox Archbishop declared,

> Some true and authentic Greeks, our fellow citizens of Athens, loyal Latin priests, wear Latin attire, while your Frenchmen "of the Greek rite" wear the attire of Orthodox priests! What confusion, what a monstrous mixture! But why do you not tell the truth? You do not differ in anything from the other subjects of the Pope of Rome, you are westerners and Latins. But for the simple Greek refugees, you pose as being "of the Greek rite," in order to show them that, in uniting with the Pope, they will keep all that they have as Orthodox, while in fact they will loose their Orthodoxy. . . . We do not consider the system of uniatism to be honest. It is a deceitful, hypocritical, and opportunistic system, a bridge leading to papism, which permits all the things that you and your subordinates are doing, and wish to do, in order to conceal your propagandistic aims.[13]

I believe that this background is important for understanding the origins of the current tensions. The Orthodox have always viewed the formation of Byzantine Catholic Churches as a sign of the hostile

---

[12] Raymond Janin, "La rebaptisation des Latins dans les Églises orthodoxes," *Annuaire de l'École des Législations religieuses* 3 (1952) 59-66.

[13] Letter of Archbishop Chrysostomos of Athens to Bishop George Calavassy of 5 July 1927, in Hiéromoine Pierre, *L'union de l'Orient avec Rome: Une controverse récente*. Orientalia Christiana Vol. XVIII. Rome: Pontifical Oriental Institute, April 1930, p. 131.

intentions of the Catholic Church towards them. They saw it as an attempt to weaken them by fomenting divisions within their communities, and as an implicit denial of their ecclesial status by the Catholic Church. As André de Halleux has observed, as a result of this policy, the fault line of the schism no longer coincides with the border between the Latin and Byzantine churches, but has moved east; the division now lies within the Byzantine Church itself.[14]

On the other hand, this same policy created Byzantine Catholic Churches which, in the course of the centuries, developed a distinct identity. Orthodox in origin, but in full communion with the Catholic Church, all of them underwent a certain process of latinization which distanced them from their Orthodox counterparts. The Byzantine Catholics formed a new reality in the Christian world, characterized by a strong loyalty both to the Byzantine patrimony and to the Bishop of Rome.

## II. The Recent Past:
### Byzantine Catholic Churches Suppressed and Restored

After the dissolution of the Austro-Hungarian Empire in the wake of World War I, the largest Byzantine Catholic Churches found themselves in new countries, mostly in Poland, Romania, and Czechoslovakia.

But it was the territorial and political changes after World War II that proved catastrophic for these Catholic Churches. The new Soviet authorities in Galicia, where the Ukrainian Catholic Church had survived under Austrian and then Polish protection, acted swiftly and ruthlessly to liquidate the church. In 1945 the entire hierarchy was imprisoned, and the following year a carefully orchestrated "synod" was held in Lviv which officially dissolved the union with Rome. All the bishops and almost half the clergy were imprisoned,

---

[14] André de Halleux, "Uniatisme et communion: Le texte catholique-orthodoxe de Freising," *Revue théologique de Louvain* 22 (1991) 19-20.

and the Ukrainian Catholics were officially absorbed into the Orthodox Church.[15]

In Romania the new communist government took similar action against the Greek Catholic Church in Transylvania. The hierarchy was imprisoned, all religious orders were dissolved, the churches were handed over to the Orthodox, and all priests who resisted the new state of affairs were banished to concentration camps.[16] The same fate awaited the smaller Byzantine Catholic Church in Slovakia. Altogether more than five million Byzantine Catholics were deprived of their religious freedom and compelled to join the local Orthodox Churches.

The question of the extent to which the Orthodox collaborated with the communists in this shameful episode has not yet been satisfactorily answered. Certainly they appeared to eagerly participate in the destruction of the Byzantine Catholic Churches as they publicly heaped praise on the dictatorships, and welcomed these erstwhile Orthodox back into the fold. But one must also take into account the strict state control to which the Orthodox were forced to submit, and the form of persecution they were subjected to. What is certain is that no deviation from the official line would have been tolerated under any circumstances. And so to distinguish what the Orthodox genuinely wanted to do from what the communists were forcing them to do is very difficult indeed, especially in view of the antipathy that the Orthodox always felt towards uniatism. It is clear that the suppression of the Byzantine Catholics by the communists for their own nefarious ends converged with long-held Orthodox aspirations to undo what they considered to be an injustice suffered long ago at the hands of the Catholic Church.

---

[15] For an account of the suppression of the Ukrainian Catholic Church, see B. Bociurkiw, "The Uniate Church in the Soviet Ukraine: A Case Study in Soviet Church Policy," *Canadian Slavonic Papers VII* (Toronto: University of Toronto Press, 1965) 89-113. Reprinted in *Ukrainian Churches Under Soviet Rule: Two Case Studies* (Cambridge, MA: Harvard University Ukrainian Studies Fund, 1984).

[16] The suppression of the Romanian Catholic Church is recounted in I. Ratiu, "The Communist Attack on the Catholic and Orthodox Churches in Romania," *Eastern Churches Quarterly* 8 (1949-1950) 163-197.

Be that as it may, the events of the 1940's convinced most Byzantine Catholics that the Orthodox Church had revealed itself as all too willing to collaborate with the forces of atheism and totalitarianism. For them, the experience of suppression only confirmed and intensified the conviction that the Orthodox Church was essentially corrupt and open to abuse by the secular authorities. This pervasive attitude of contempt would come to the surface, and clash with Orthodox sentiments about uniatism when these churches resurfaced after the collapse of communism.

The fortunes of the Byzantine Catholics began to change with the accession of Mikhail Gorbachev to the post of General Secretary of the Communist Party of the Soviet Union in March 1985. As soon as its legal status was recognized, the Ukrainian Catholic Church made a dramatic recovery.[17] The process was expedited by the local Ukrainian government, which also facilitated the return of churches to the Ukrainian Catholics.

The Moscow Patriarchate protested, however, that in some cases violence was being used in the reclaiming of these churches, a charge the Catholics denied. A high-level meeting between officials of the Vatican and the Moscow Patriarchate was held in Moscow in January 1990 to discuss these problems. A document was approved which made recommendations in view of a resolution of the conflict.[18] A joint commission was set up to examine specific cases of disputed church property, but it was abandoned among mutual recriminations at its first meeting. In the meantime, the Byzantine Catholic resurgence continued, and by the end of 1991, the Orthodox

---

[17] See B. Bociurkiw, "The Ukrainian Catholic Church in the USSR under Gorbachev," *Problems of Communism* 39 (November-December 1990) 1-19.

[18] "Recommendations for the Normalization of Relations Between Orthodox and Catholics of the Eastern Rite in the Western Ukraine," *Information Service* 71 (1989/III-IV). 131-133. Archbishop Edward Idris Cassidy, President of the Pontifical Council for Promoting Christian Unity, provided background in his "Vatican-Orthodox Reach Accord on Ukrainian Issue," *L'Osservatore Romano* [Weekly English Edition] 5 March 1990. The document was also published in *The Journal of the Moscow Patriarchate*, 1990, n. 5, pp. 8-9.

presence in western Ukraine had almost vanished,[19] a process which the Moscow Patriarchate denounced as evidence of Catholic proselytism.

In Romania, one of the first acts of the National Salvation Front after the overthrow of the Ceauşescu regime in December 1989 was to annul the 1948 decree which had dissolved the Greek Catholic Church. But it did not provide for the return of the Greek Catholic church buildings to their previous owners. This set the stage for a confrontation between Greek Catholics and Orthodox which has still not been resolved.[20]

The Romanian Greek Catholics sum up their position in the phrase *restitutio in integrum*: they demand that all the property confiscated in 1948 be returned as a matter of justice, and present this as a pre-condition to any sort of dialogue with the Romanian Orthodox Church.[21] But the Orthodox insist that the demographic situation has shifted significantly in the past four decades, and that the present pastoral needs of the two communities must be taken into account. They proposed the redistribution of churches on the basis of a census and the deliberations of a joint commission. Such a census was taken in January 1992, and the outcome was announced in May.[22] But the Greek Catholics did not accept the results, according to which they were now only 1% of the population (228,377), a small fraction of the 1.5 million faithful they had at the time of the suppression. In fact, very few churches have been returned, and the Greek Catholics have had to begin a program of building new places of worship.

---

[19] The only significant Orthodox presence remaining in the region was that of the Ukrainian Autocephalous Orthodox Church which is considered uncanonical by the Moscow Patriarchate and other Orthodox Churches.

[20] D. Ionescu, "The Orthodox-Uniate Conflict," *Report on Eastern Europe*, 2 August 1991, pp. 29-34.

[21] The Greek Catholic stance was set forth by T. Langa in "Poziţia noastră," *Viaţa creştina* n. 1 (February 1990) and n. 11 (July 1990).

[22] "Aceasta este România," *Adevărul*, 30-31 May 1991. For analysis see Michael Shafir, "Preliminary Results of the 1992 Romanian Census," *RFE/RL Research Report* 1/30 (24 July 1992) 62-68.

*III. The International Commission for Dialogue*

Events such as these were bound to have an effect on the work of the International Commission for Dialogue between the Catholic and Orthodox Churches. But before examining the work of the commission, it would be good to take a brief look at the sea change in attitudes between Catholics and Orthodox that began in the 1960's.

For Catholics, the convocation of the Second Vatican Council at which Orthodox observers were present marked a new beginning. A positive evaluation of the Eastern tradition is found in the Council documents, especially *Unitatis Redintegratio*. Most importantly, it clearly states that the Orthodox are "churches" in the full sense of the word, and that they have valid sacraments. This would lay the foundation for the development of an ecclesiology of communion and the notion that Catholics and Orthodox are "sister churches."

This coincided with the development of what became known as the "dialogue of charity," a kind of learning to trust one another again, a process that had to take place before any fruitful theological dialogue could begin. In January 1964 Pope Paul VI and Patriarch Athenagoras of Constantinople met for the first time, in Jerusalem. On December 7, 1965 in Rome and Istanbul they simultaneously proclaimed the lifting of the mutual excommunications of 1054, declaring them "erased from the memory" of the church.[23]

All this was the prelude to the establishment of the theological commission by Pope John Paul II and Patriarch Dimitrios I of Constantinople in 1979. Its first ten years of work reflected the growing consensus between the two communions, and saw the publication of three agreed statements on such issues as the relationship between the Trinity, the Church and Eucharist; the sacraments

---

[23] On the events and theological developments leading up to the dialogue, see Dimitri Salachas, "Il dialogo teologico ufficiale tra la chiesa cattolico-romana e la chiesa ortodossa: iter e documentazione," *Quaderni di O Odigos* 2/1 (1986) 7-96.

of initiation and the connection between common faith and sacra-mental communion; and the theology of the ordained ministry.[24]

But while all this was going on, the issue of uniatism continued to fester in the background. The largest Eastern Catholic Churches were still illegal and, to a large extent, theologically frozen in the 1940's because of their isolation and persecution. And the Orthodox contin-ued to express their strong opposition not only to the policy of uniatism, but also to the very existence of these churches. In fact, some Orthodox theologians, especially in Greece, called for the "abandonment of uniatism" by the Catholic Church before a theo-logical dialogue could begin.[25] Once it did begin, there were objec-tions to the presence of any Byzantines in the Catholic delegation. And even after the dialogue was in progress, some Orthodox mem-bers still called for this issue to be treated by the commission with urgency.[26]

There was a general feeling, however, that the commission was not prepared to deal with this issue. A programmatic document adopted by the preparatory commission in 1978 had called for the commission to begin with elements that the two churches held in common. Only after a solid consensus had been attained on those basic elements was it recommended that controversial points such as papal primacy and uniatism be addressed.

But the events following the revolutions of 1989 pushed this question to the forefront. The Orthodox felt threatened by what they saw as a resurgence of uniatism and Catholic proselytism. This is why, when the Sixth Plenary of the dialogue met at Freising, Germany, in June 1990, the Orthodox delegates insisted that the topic already prepared for discussion be set aside and that the

---

[24] For an overview of the commission's work see Paul McPartlan, "Towards Catholic-Orthodox Unity," *Communio* 19 (Summer 1992) 305-320.

[25] Metropolitan Chrysostomos of Peristerion, "A Problem and an Appeal: A Necessary Presupposition for the beginning and the success of the Theological Dialogue between the Orthodox and Roman Catholic Churches," Θεολογία 50 (1979) 856-868.

[26] Metropolitan Chrysostomos of Peristerion, "Le dialogue théologique des Eglises orthodoxe et catholique-romaine," Θεολογία 57 (1986) 329-342.

question of the origins of uniatism and the present status of the Byzantine Catholic Churches be addressed to the exclusion of all else.

The statement issued at the end of the Freising meeting bears the hallmarks of hasty preparation.[27] Given the circumstances, this was unavoidable. Nevertheless, it made some important assertions. First, it affirmed the principle of religious freedom, and thus the right of the Byzantine Catholic Churches to exist. It also rejected "uniatism," which it defined as a policy used in the past to achieve unity with the Orthodox by detaching Orthodox communities from their mother churches, and uniting them with the Catholic Church. This was "a method of unity opposed to the common Tradition of our churches," and inconsistent with a sister-church ecclesiology. Thus "it would be regretful" to return to this policy, given the progress towards unity that had already been achieved.[28] Although it is provisional in nature, the Freising statement remains the only official joint statement on this problem. A few months later the Orthodox members of the commission, meeting in Istanbul, referred to it as "the only positive sign regarding the issue at hand."

At Freising the commission realized that further study was needed, and set in motion an extensive examination of the issue. The result was a working document drafted by the dialogue's coordinating committee at Ariccia, near Rome, in June 1991.

Although the Ariccia text was not intended for publication, it has nevertheless appeared in several languages.[29] Its title, "Uniatism as a Method of Union in the Past, and the Present Search for Full

---

[27] André de Halleux in his "Uniatisme et communion" cited in note 14 provides a detailed analysis of the Freising text.

[28] "Sixth Plenary Meeting of the Joint International Commission for Theological Dialogue between the Roman Catholic Church and the Orthodox Church," *Information Service* 73 (1990/II) 52-53. Quotes from number 6.

[29] English: *The Journal of the Moscow Patriarchate* (1991) Nr. 10, 60-62 (also in Russian edition); Greek: "Κρίσιμη φάση του διαλόγου Καθολικῶν καὶ Ὀρθοδόξων," *Καθολικὴ*, 23 July 1991 (the Catholic newspaper in Athens); French: "«Le Document d'Ariccia» L'uniatisme, méthode d'union du passé, et recherche actuelle de la pleine communion," *Irénikon* 65 (1992) 491-498.

Communion," points to its basic thesis: while the policy of uniatism is rejected as pertaining to a past stage in relations between Catholics and Orthodox, today's search for reconciliation must continue, making use of new methods.

The document briefly treats the historical development of the Byzantine Catholic Churches and acknowledges that as a method to achieve unity between East and West uniatism failed: ". . . the division persists, embittered by these attempts" (n. 4). The Ariccia text also notes the subsequent development, first in the Catholic Church, and then in the Orthodox Church as a reaction, of an ecclesiology in which each church viewed itself as possessing the exclusive means of salvation. Thus the conversion of others to one's own Church came to be considered necessary for salvation. This view paved the way for violations of religious freedom and even the use of force to compel Eastern Catholics to return to the church of their forefathers.

But the document also observes that this situation changed radically after the Pan-Orthodox Conferences and the Second Vatican Council. Now, neither Catholics nor Orthodox can consider themselves as Church in an exclusive sense. Consequently, the Orthodox and Catholic Churches have a joint responsibility for "keeping the Church of God in faithfulness to the divine plan, especially concerning unity."

The Ariccia text affirms that the realization of unity must be a common endeavor of the two churches to attain full agreement on the content of the faith (n. 9). Once this is achieved, the Catholic and Orthodox Churches will restore full communion, and the problems posed by the Eastern Catholic Churches will have been eliminated. Dialogue is pointed to as the only means by which this goal can be attained. The first section of the document concludes by citing the rejection of all forms of proselytism by Pope John Paul II and Patriarch Dimitrios of Constantinople in their joint declaration of 7 December 1987.

The second section of the Ariccia document is a series of concrete recommendations suggested for the situation in Eastern Europe. The Catholic Church is encouraged to find ways in which the Byzantine

Catholic Churches can contribute to the process of reconciliation. The Orthodox, for their part, are called upon to accept the assurances of the Catholic Church that it does not wish to expand at the expense of the Orthodox East, and that it has abandoned proselytism among the Orthodox faithful.

Again, this is a working text . . . it is not an official document produced by the international dialogue. It was to have been considered at the seventh plenary meeting in Lebanon last June, but it had to be postponed when it was learned that eight of the fourteen Orthodox Churches would not be present. The meeting is now due to take place next June in Lebanon.

When examining the documents produced by the international commission, it is essential that one point be clearly understood. While it has rejected uniatism as a method for achieving unity between Catholics and Orthodox today, it has in no way called into question the existence of the Byzantine Catholic Churches. This is a crucial distinction which has been lost on some commentators.[30] In these documents "uniatism" is a technical term which refers only to a policy, a method of reconciling Catholics and Orthodox that was used in the past. The term "Uniate" is not normally used in reference to today's Byzantine Catholic Churches because it is considered derogatory. By way of illustration of what the commission is doing, one could imagine that the method used in the formation of the Church of England under Henry VIII might well be rejected as inappropriate to today's relationship between Catholics and Anglicans. But such a rejection does not imply that the Church of England has no right to exist, or a positive role to play.

It would not do justice to conclude this overview of current developments without also mentioning a document that was issued by the Vatican's «Pro Russia» Commission on 1 June 1992. This docu-

---

[30] For instance see Serge Kelleher, "Church in the Middle: Greek-Catholics in Central and Eastern Europe," *Religion, State and Society* 20 (1992) 289-302. Kelleher's definition of uniatism as "the anomalous existence of churches of the Eastern Orthodox tradition which are nevertheless attached to the western church" (p. 298) causes him to misunderstand the meaning of the Freising statement.

ment, which was drafted largely in response to Orthodox concerns, is entitled, "General Principles and Practical Norms for Coordinating the Evangelizing Activity and Ecumenical Commitment of the Catholic Church in Russia and in the Other Countries of the Commonwealth of Independent States (CIS)."[31]

The first section of the text has to do with general principles. The document affirms that the Catholic Church's claim to have a right to provide for the pastoral care of its own faithful should not be seen as a way of entering into competition with the Russian Orthodox Church. The ecumenical dimension of Catholic mission activity in those countries must be a pastoral priority. Indeed, because of their common heritage, "Catholics and Orthodox can bear common witness to Christ before a world which yearns for its own unity."

The «Pro Russia» document goes on to state that Catholic activities in traditionally Orthodox countries must be conducted in ways which take this heritage fully into account. The Byzantine and Armenian traditions are to be held in special esteem, and Catholics should promote cooperation with the Orthodox wherever possible.

Practical directives are given in the second section. The Catholic authorities are asked to provide for an ecumenical formation for their clergy and to promote a climate of trust and peaceful cooperation. They should also ensure that no Catholic activity appear to establish "parallel structures of evangelization" over against the Orthodox. All Catholics involved in the apostolate in those countries are asked to work under the close supervision of the Catholic bishops.

The «Pro Russia» Commission also instructs Catholic authorities to inform local Orthodox bishops of all their important pastoral initiatives, especially the opening of new parishes. And in a key

---

31 English translation in *Origins* 22/17 (8 October 1992) 301-304. French: *Plamia* 85 (Christmas 1992) 39-47 and *La documentation catholique* 2056 (6 & 20 September 1992) 786-790. A Greek translation was published in the 21 and 28 July 1992 issues of *Καθολική* (Athens). Italian: "Direttive per l'apostolato cattolico nell'ex Unione Sovietica, *La Civiltà Cattolica* 3415 (3 October 1992) 66-75. Slightly edited versions of the document were published in both the English and French editions of *Ecumenism* [Montreal] 107 (September 1992).

passage the document even states that Catholic pastors should "endeavor to cooperate with the Orthodox bishops in developing pastoral initiatives of the Orthodox Church. They should be pleased if by their contribution they can help to train good Christians" (n. 4).

Although the «Pro Russia» text is now available to the public in several languages, it is regrettable that its impact has been somewhat limited by the fact that it has not been published by an official organ of the Holy See. Nevertheless, in my view, this is the most helpful and positive set of guidelines which the Vatican has promulgated so far on the subject of Catholic-Orthodox relations. It should do much to allay Orthodox fears with regard to true Catholic intentions in the region. It is soundly based on an ecclesiology of communion and respects the ecclesial nature of the Orthodox Churches, as well as the priority they enjoy in their historic homelands.

All this shows that progress has been made towards reducing the tensions between Catholics and Orthodox that flared up in the wake of the collapse of European communism that began in 1989. Nevertheless, the fact that some Orthodox Churches have expressed reservations about continuing the theological dialogue, and the question mark that still hangs over its next session, indicate that we're not out of the woods yet. For the wounds of history are rarely forgotten in these regions. As an English observer of the Balkans wrote some 85 years ago, "Assuredly there is something in the spirit of the East which is singularly kindly to survivals and anachronisms. The centuries do not follow one another, they coexist. There is no lopping of withered customs, no burial of dead ideas."[32]

## IV. Challenges for the Future

So what are the prospects for significant progress towards improving relations between Catholics and Orthodox? What challenges do the two churches face on the path towards full reconciliation? I

---

[32] H.N. Brailsford, *Macedonia: Its Races and Their Future* (1906), quoted by Duncan M. Perry in "The Republic of Macedonia and the Odds for Survival," *RFE/RL Research Report* 1/46 (20 November 1992) 12.

would now like to turn to some of the major issues the two churches will have to face.

First, the Orthodox. The Orthodox Churches in Eastern and Central Europe are having to adjust to radical changes in their societies. In some cases these changes have triggered serious internal problems within the local churches. For example, in Bulgaria there has been a schism in the synod of bishops over the legitimacy of the election of Patriarch Maxim while the communists were in power.[33] The Churches of Serbia and Georgia are preoccupied by the wars in which their faithful are involved. The Orthodox Church in the republic of Moldova has split between two rival jurisdictions dependent on Moscow and Bucharest.[34] And many of these churches have been hit hard by the catastrophic economic conditions in their countries.

Other changes are altering the shape of the Orthodox world. Perhaps the most significant of these is the decision of the Moscow Patriarchate to grant autonomy to the Orthodox Churches in the new countries that have risen from the ashes of the Soviet Union. This rank has been granted to the Orthodox Churches in Moldova, Estonia, Latvia, Belarus, and Ukraine. It is not unthinkable that this development heralds the dismemberment of the Moscow Patriarchate. But even if these new churches remain autonomous and not fully independent, they may claim the right to participate in pan-Orthodox activities, just as the autonomous Orthodox Church of Finland now does. In this case, the overall makeup of pan-Orthodox commissions would be altered decisively in a Slavic direction.

The Orthodox are also faced with the continuing problem of the canonical recognition of churches which have unilaterally asserted their administrative independence. Among these are the "Macedonian Orthodox Church" in the former Yugoslav republic, and the "Ukrainian Autocephalous Orthodox Church" which does not recognize any link with the Moscow Patriarchate. In the present

---

[33] Kjell Engelbrekt, "Bulgaria's Religious Institutions under Fire," *RFE/RL Research Report* 1/38 (25 September 1992) 61-62.

[34] See *Service Orthodoxe de Presse* 175 (February 1993) 12-15.

state of affairs, sizable numbers of Orthodox faithful are technically in a state of schism from the Orthodox Church as a whole.

All this shows that the Orthodox world is going through a period marked by the greatest transformations seen in this century. It is fortuitous at this crucial juncture that vigorous leadership is being provided by the new Patriarch of Constantinople, Bartholomew I, and that he is devoting his formidable energies to solving these internal problems. We must wish him well, because only a united and self-confident Orthodoxy will be able to engage the other churches in sustained and successful dialogue.

The Orthodox are presented with a special challenge in their relations with the Catholic Church. Many of them perceive this church as vast in size, with huge resources, and disposing of a highly efficient organizational structure. When this is coupled with their historical consciousness of being the victim of Catholic aggression which they blame for divisions within their own ranks, many Orthodox become fearful of entering into serious dialogue with Rome. It is this fear which explains why some Orthodox still tend to blame the Vatican for such internal problems as the schism in the Bulgarian Orthodox Holy Synod or the attempt of the Macedonian Orthodox Church to gain autocephalous status. What is needed is greater trust in the expressed intentions of the Catholic Church, a trust which can only be gained by careful study of post-Vatican II developments, and greater direct experience of Catholic ecclesial life. The Orthodox Churches need trained individuals who know the Catholic Church first-hand, and who can counter misguided stereotypes and unfounded fears.

It will also be very important for the Orthodox to try to find ways to promote a positive relationship with the Byzantine Catholic Churches. The tendency to view them as artificial creations which even now exist only because they are propped up by the Vatican is very destructive, and does not do justice to their centuries-long struggle for survival, sometimes even in the face of Latin Catholic hostility. While one can appreciate Orthodox feelings about the methods used in the formation of some of these churches, the most fundamental principles of religious freedom, not to speak of the

Gospel, require that they be accorded the respect and, yes, even love, due to fellow Christians. Moreover, relations between Orthodox and Byzantine Catholics do not have to be hostile. In other parts of the world such as the Americas and the Middle East,[35] where relations could develop freely after Vatican II, there is often a downright friendly atmosphere between Byzantine Catholics and Orthodox. This gives reason to hope that with the passing of time, a similar situation will develop in Eastern and Central Europe.

But for this to happen, the Orthodox will need to come to terms with the role they played in the suffering that Byzantine Catholics experienced under communism. Many are scandalized by the way in which some Orthodox continue to defend the communist-inspired "synods" of the late 1940's which sanctioned the forceful liquidation of several Byzantine Catholic Churches. Only if the Orthodox squarely face up to those events will it be possible to develop a positive relationship between these two groups.

But the Catholic Church also faces daunting challenges. It can be convincingly argued that in the new situation in Eastern and Central Europe, the Catholic Church stands to gain more than any other denomination.[36] In general, Catholics display a higher religiosity than any other group in the region. They also have access to financial and other resources from fellow Catholics in the West, an advantage that the Orthodox do not have. This means that the Catholic Church is very well positioned not only to retrieve the status it held in those countries before the advent of communism, but also to expand if it wishes.

This would, however, be a foolhardy course of action. While the Catholic Church might gain a larger share of the Christians in those countries, such nations as Russia, Romania, Bulgaria and Serbia are going to remain basically Orthodox. Moreover, entering into competition with those Orthodox Churches would run counter to the

---

[35] For example, on the situation in Aleppo, Syria, see Ignace Dick, "Les relations interchrétiennes à Alep: Comment est vécu l'oecuménisme dans une grande métropole syrienne?" *Proche Orient Chrétien* 39 (1989) 113-126.

[36] Sabrina P. Ramet asserts that this is the case in "The New Church-State Configuration in Eastern Europe," *East European Politics and Societies* 5 (1991) 247.

implications of the teachings of the Second Vatican Council and the expressed desire of Pope John Paul II, who has repeatedly stated that Catholics are not to proselytize among the Orthodox faithful.[37] The Catholic Church has opted for dialogue with the Orthodox East as the only method which corresponds to the sister church relationship which has evolved since the Second Vatican Council. It is only this method which respects the Orthodox precisely as churches, and engages the legitimate ecclesial structures by which they are governed.

There are certain aspects of this commitment, however, which remain to be fleshed out. For it requires a new way of thinking on the part of those who are accustomed to providing for the needs of local Catholic churches without considering the impact such actions might have on Orthodox churches present in the same region.

It is here that the question of the establishment of Catholic diocesan structures in the former communist countries comes in. When Catholic hierarchies were reestablished there, the local Russian and Romanian Orthodox Churches protested strongly not only that the new structures exceeded the pastoral needs of the local Catholic faithful, but also that they had been presented with a *fait accompli*, not having been consulted in the decision-making process. Many Orthodox feared that this indicated the beginning of renewed Catholic proselytism in their countries. I believe that the reality was precisely the opposite: the setting in place of Catholic bishops with pastoral authority was intended partially as a way of stemming the enthusiasm of certain Catholic free-lance groups who were intent on evangelizing the East, groups who either were not aware of the new attitudes towards the Orthodox or who simply disregarded them. The guidelines of the «Pro Russia» document hint that this is the case. Nevertheless, the time when the Catholic Church can make major decisions concerning its activity in an Orthodox country without input from the local Orthodox Church is over. If these are truly

---

[37] See the Pope's speech in the Orthodox Church at Bialystok, Poland, on 5 June 1991 in *Information Service* 77 (1991/II) 40.

churches in the theological sense of the term, they must at least be consulted before such decisions are taken.

The role the Byzantine Catholic Churches can play in relation to the Orthodox remains a difficult question. The very deep-seated Orthodox animosity towards these churches makes it difficult for them to make a positive contribution. Moreover, the Byzantine Catholics in Central and Eastern Europe are emerging from a lengthy period of isolation from the rest of the Catholic Church, and are only now beginning to assimilate the new Catholic attitudes to the ecumenical movement in general and to the Orthodox in particular. It is urgent that ways be found to facilitate this process which both respect the dignity of these churches and avoid patronizing attitudes. Resources need to be made available to Byzantine Catholics of those regions enabling them to send theology students to the West, for example, and to promote exchanges with the rest of the Catholic Church at every level.

But the Catholic Church has now reached a point where it must not only consider ways of assisting its own people in those regions, but the Orthodox as well. The «Pro Russia» document encourages Catholics to cooperate in Orthodox pastoral initiatives, to assist the Orthodox Church to re-evangelize its own people. What would have been unthinkable twenty-five years ago has now become official policy. But in general the concrete modes of applying this principle remain to be worked out.

Both Catholics and Orthodox in Europe, then, are presented with the challenge of learning to find new ways of relating which correspond to the increasingly explicit recognition of each another as sister churches. This will not be easy, and yet it is of the greatest importance. For at the present juncture of European history, the future development of the relationship between East and West stands at a crossroads. It is by no means clear that the countries of Eastern Europe will slavishly embrace the economic and cultural systems of the West; they might well be ill-advised to do so. But the question which remains to be answered is whether or not these countries will enter into a mutually beneficial exchange with the West, or retreat into an isolationist and perhaps even fascist system which would present untold dangers for the security of the continent.

Along these lines, the greatest enigma remains Russia. The dissolution of the USSR, the collapse of the economy, the specter of hyperinflation, the presence of some 25 million Russians in the new foreign countries of the "near abroad," and a sense of national humiliation; all these things have converged to cause Russians to seriously question their nation's identity and future role in the world. The intellectual debate on this issue has crystallized around three basic groups: the "westernizers" who advocate close contacts with the West and the evolution of Russia into a democracy on the West European model; the "isolationists" who want Russia to have only minimal contact with other countries and focus on internal problems; and the "imperialists" or "unionists" who wish to see the reestablishment of a Eurasian confederation on the territory of the old USSR.[38] This last group, which seems to be gaining in strength, is staunchly anti-democratic and anti-western in its views.[39] Thus the outcome of the current struggle between these groups could have enormous ramifications for the rest of Europe.

At the same time, there is mounting evidence of a deep thirst among the Russian people for spiritual values. A survey conducted in April and May 1992 revealed that some 74% of Russians questioned wanted to live their lives according to a set of essential values, and at least 70% wanted a more spiritual content in their lives.[40] A similar survey conducted in October 1992 showed that, while there was profound dissatisfaction with the current political situation, the institution in the country which enjoyed the highest level of confidence among the people was the church.[41]

---

[38] Vera Tolz, "Russia: Westernizers Continue to Challenge National Patriots," *RFE/RL Research Report* 1/49 (11 December 1992) 1-9.

[39] Igor Torbakov, "The 'Statists' and the Ideology of Russian Imperial Nationalism," *RFE/RL Research Report* 1/49 (11 December 1992) 10-16.

[40] Mark Rhodes, "Russians' Spiritual Values," *RFE/RL Research Report* 1/41 (16 October 1992) 64-65.

[41] Mark Rhodes, "Political Attitudes in Russia," *RFE/RL Research Report* 2/3 (15 January 1993) 42-44.

When these facts are considered alongside the present rebirth of the Russian Orthodox Church, which is expanding rapidly in every area of church life, it is easy to see what a crucial role the church will play in determining the final direction that Russia will take. If the Russian Church decides that contacts with the West are futile or even dangerous, it will tend to push Russians in the direction of the old imperialism which poses so many perils. But if the theological exchange and other contacts produce real fruit, generating greater confidence and trust between the Orthodox and the churches of the West, the Moscow Patriarchate could play a leading role in encouraging Russia to follow a parallel path.

The challenges, therefore, are great, and much hangs in the balance. But ultimately, whatever the political and social ramifications of better relations between the Orthodox and Catholic churches, the final goal of unity remains a Christian imperative which corresponds to nothing less than the will of Christ himself. These two sister churches, long embittered by the misunderstandings and wounds of the past, are experiencing the rekindling of an ancient love. In doing so, and in responding in creative ways to the challenges posed by the process of reconciliation, the unity of our world will be strengthened, and God will be praised.

March 18, 1993

# Appendix II

## The Contemporary Relationship between
## The Catholic and Oriental Orthodox Churches

"The Oriental Orthodox Churches" is a term which is generally used today to refer to a communion of five independent ancient eastern churches.[1] The common element among them is their non-reception of the christological teachings of the Council of Chalcedon which was celebrated in 451.[2] These churches are the Armenian Apostolic Church,[3] the Coptic Orthodox Church, the Ethiopian Orthodox Church, the Syrian Orthodox Church, and the Malankara Orthodox Syrian Church in India.[4] All are members of the World Council of Churches and have committed themselves to the contem-

---

[1] The Assyrian Church of the East, descended from the ancient East Syrian or "Nestorian" Church which rejected the christological teachings of the Council of Ephesus in 431, is not included in this study, although it is at times incorrectly referred to as one of the Oriental Orthodox Churches. Because of its christological tradition, the Assyrian Church is not in communion with any other church.

[2] See W. de Vries, "The Reasons for the Rejection of the Council of Chalcedon by the Oriental Orthodox Churches," *Wort und Wahrheit*, Supplementary Issue No. 1 (Vienna: Herder, 1972) 54-60.

[3] The Armenian Apostolic Church is made up of two distinct Catholicosates which are separate members of the World Council of Churches. The Catholicosate of Etchmiadzin, in the former Soviet republic of Armenia, is recognized as the first see. The Catholicosate of Cilicia is based at Antelias, Lebanon. In addition, two Armenian Patriarchates in Istanbul and Jerusalem are autonomous churches dependent on Etchmiadzin.

[4] The Malankara Orthodox Syrian Church is autocephalous and includes about half of the total 2,000,000 Oriental Orthodox faithful in India. The other half makes up the autonomous Malankara Syrian Orthodox Church, which is dependent upon the Syrian Orthodox Patriarchate in Damascus.

porary ecumenical movement. In total, there are probably about thirty million Oriental Orthodox faithful in the world today.[5]

In the 1960's, these churches began a process of rapprochement with both the Catholic and Orthodox[6] Churches. This paper examines their renewed relationship with the Catholic Church, which took place through unofficial theological consultations, visits between popes and hierarchs ' of these churches, and official theological dialogues with the Coptic Orthodox and Malankara Orthodox Syrian Churches. It begins with a chronological presentation of the way in which the ancient christological dispute has been addressed, and shows how major progress has been made as a result of the symbiotic relationship that developed between theologians meeting in unofficial consultations and church leaders. The second section focusses on ecclesiology where, in spite of the mutual recognition of each other as churches, significant divergences remain to be resolved.

## Christology

The Oriental Orthodox said little about christology in their earliest encounters with Pope Paul VI. But the Pope seems to have been convinced that the ancient disputes over christological terminology should no longer prevent the two churches from professing their

---

[5] See membership statistics provided in Ans J. vander Bent, ed., *Handbook Member Churches World Council of Churches*, Fully Revised Edition (Geneva: WCC, 1985).

[6] I use the term "Orthodox" without the adjective"Oriental" to refer to the Orthodox Churches of the Byzantine tradition which are in communion with the Patriarch of Constantinople, whom they recognize as a point of unity. On relations between the Oriental Orthodox and Orthodox Churches see André de Halleux, "Actualité du néochalcédonisme: Un accord christologique récent entre Orthodoxes," *Revue théologique de Louvain* 21 (1990) 32-54, and Paulos Gregorios, William Lazareth, Nikos Nissiotis, eds. *Does Chalcedon Divide or Unite? Towards Convergence in Orthodox Christology* (Geneva: World Council of Churches, 1981).

faith in Christ together.[7] In his welcoming speech to Armenian Catholicos Khoren I of Cilicia in May 1967, Pope Paul said:

> With you We give glory to the one God, Father, Son, and Holy Spirit; with you We acclaim Jesus Christ, Son of God, Incarnate Word, our Redeemer, the founder and head of the holy Church, his mystical body.[8]

During his visit to Armenian Patriarch of Constantinople Shnork Kalustian in July 1967, Pope Paul pointed out the importance of the teaching of the Council of Ephesus as the basis of the unity of the two churches:

> It is a great consolation to meditate upon the vision of Christ presented to the Church and to the world by that holy assembly. That vision, too, we share in common. God, made man for our salvation, is the God we confess in our Creed and preach to the world.[9]

And in his speech to Armenian Catholicos Vasken I (Etchmiadzin) in May 1970, Pope Paul stated that the different expressions of the one faith are due in large part to non-theological factors:

> If we have come to divergent expressions of the central mystery of our faith because of unfortunate circumstances, cultural differences and the difficulty of translating terms worked out with much effort and given precise statement only gradually, then research into these doctrinal difficulties must be undertaken again in order to understand what has brought them about and to be able to overcome them in a brotherly way.[10]

The Pope went on to quote Nerses IV, a 12th century Armenian Catholicos, who wrote that the term "two natures" would be accept-

---

[7] From the Catholic point of view, the idea that the dispute was essentially a question of terminology had been officially expressed as early as 1951, when Pope Pius XII stated in his encyclical *Sempiternus Rex* that these Christians "verbis praecipue a recto tramite deflectere videantur" ("seem to depart from the right path chiefly in words"). *Acta Apostolicae Sedis* 43 (1951) 636.

[8] *Acta Apostolicae Sedis* 59 (1967) 510.

[9] *Information Service* [Secretariat for Promoting Christian Unity] 3 (1967/3) 13.

[10] *Information Service* 11 (1970/III) 5-6.

able insofar as it indicates the absence of any confusion of humanity and divinity in Christ, against Eutyches and Apollinaris. Pope Paul then asked: "Has the time not come to clear up once and for all such misunderstandings inherited from the past?"[11]

In the *Common Declaration* signed at the end of Vasken's visit, a clear commitment was made by both churches to encourage theological research into the remaining difficulties:

> They exhort theologians to devote themselves to a common study leading to a deepening of their understanding of the mystery of our Lord Jesus Christ and of the revelation brought about in him. . . . For their part, the Pope and the Catholicos will try to do all that is possible to support these efforts and will give them their pastoral blessing.[12]

The *Pro Oriente* foundation in Vienna took up this challenge and sponsored a historic series of discussions between theologians of the two communions. The first "Non-Official Ecumenical Consultation between Theologians of the Oriental Orthodox and the Roman Catholic Churches" took place in Vienna in September 1971. In the communiqué issued at the end of the meeting, the theologians affirmed that a common basis had been found in the apostolic traditions and the first three Ecumenical Councils. After rejecting both Eutychian and Nestorian christologies, they expressed their common faith in Christ in these words:

> We believe that our Lord and Saviour, Jesus Christ, is God the Son Incarnate; perfect in his divinity and perfect in his humanity. His divinity was not separated from his humanity for a single moment, not for the twinkling of an eye. His humanity is one with his divinity without commixtion, without confusion, without division, without separation. We in our common faith in the one Lord Jesus Christ, regard his mystery inexhaustible and ineffable and for the human mind never fully comprehensible or expressible.

---

[11] Ibid., 6.

[12] *Acta Apostolicae Sedis* 62 (1970) 416.

We see that there are still differences in the theological interpretation of the mystery of Christ because of our different ecclesiastical and theological traditions; we are convinced, however, that these differing formulations on both sides can be understood along the lines of the faith of Nicea and Ephesus.[13]

This text reveals an effort to avoid terminology which had been the focus of ancient disputes. Indeed, the words "person" and "nature" never appear. It is an effort to create a new vocabulary, using new concepts to express the one faith which underlies both traditional formulations.

The importance of this theological breakthrough was quickly realized. When the Syrian Patriarch Ignatius Yacoub III visited Rome one month later, Pope Paul was already echoing the findings of the *Pro Oriente* meeting when he said that theologians discussing the issue

> are convinced . . . that these various formulations can be understood along the lines of the early councils, which is the faith we also profess.[14]

This was also reflected in the *Common Declaration* which was signed at the end of the Patriarch's visit:

> Progress has already been made and Pope Paul VI and the Patriarch Mar Ignatius III are in agreement that there is no difference in the faith they profess concerning the mystery of the Word of God made flesh and become really man, even if over the centuries difficulties have arisen out of the different theological expressions by which this faith was expressed.[15]

---

[13] "Communiqué," *Wort und Wahrheit*, Supplementary Issue No. 1 (Vienna: Herder, 1972) 182.

[14] *Information Service* 16 (1972/I) 3.

[15] *Acta Apostolicae Sedis* 63 (1971) 814.

In May 1973 Coptic Pope[16] Shenouda III visited Pope Paul VI in Rome. The profession of faith contained in the *Common Declaration* they signed at the end of the meeting clearly benefited from the *Pro Oriente* formulation:

> We confess that our Lord and God and Saviour and King of us all, Jesus Christ, is perfect God with respect to His divinity, perfect man with respect to His humanity. In Him His divinity is united with His humanity in a real, perfect union without mingling, without commixtion, without confusion, without alteration, without division, without separation. His divinity did not separate from His humanity for an instant, not for the twinkling of an eye. He who is God eternal and invisible became visible in the flesh, and took upon Himself the form of a servant. In Him are preserved all the properties of the divinity and all the properties of the humanity, together in a real, perfect, indivisible and insepa-rable union.[17]

Despite the historic nature of this joint christological declaration, the theologians involved in the *Pro Oriente* consultations realized that more progress could be made. Christology, then, still figured strongly in their discussions at the second meeting which took place in September, 1973. In the final communiqué, the theologians of both communions built on what had been said in the 1971 statement. They added that the mystery of Christ is incomprehensible, and that all concepts about him are limited. Thus correct christological formu-lations can be wrongly understood, and behind an apparently wrong formulation there can be a right understanding. This enabled them to affirm that

> the definition of the Council of Chalcedon, rightly understood today, affirms the unity of person and the indissoluble union of

---

[16] The Coptic Patriarchs of Alexandria have had the title "Pope" since ancient times. His full title is "Pope and Patriarch of the Great City of Alexandria and of all Egypt, the Middle East, Ethiopia, Nubia, and the Pentapolis."

[17] *Acta Apostolicae Sedis* 65 (1973) 300.

Godhead and Manhood in Christ despite the phrase "in two natures."[18]

The statement also deals with problems of terminology:

> For those of us in the Western tradition, to hear of the one nature
> of Christ can be misleading, because it may be misunderstood as a
> denial of his humanity. For those of us in the Oriental Orthodox
> Churches to hear of two natures can be misleading because it can
> be misunderstood as affirming two persons in Christ. But both
> sides agree in rejecting Eutychianism and Nestorianism . . .
>
> Our common effort to clarify the meaning of the Greek terms *hy-
> postasis* and *physis* in the Trinitarian and Christological contexts
> made us realize how difficult it was to find a satisfactory defini-
> tion of these terms that could do justice to both contexts in a con-
> sistent manner.[19]

The communiqué also calls for new terminology which would express more effectively the mystery of Christ for people today.

Since 1973, Popes and heads of Oriental Orthodox Churches have
affirmed repeatedly that they share the same faith in Christ. Indeed,
this seems taken for granted in most statements. For instance, during
his visit to Rome in June 1983, Moran Mar Baselius Marthoma
Mathews I, the Catholicos of the Malankara Orthodox Syrian Church
of India, quoted Cyril of Alexandria's "one divine-human nature"
formula as being part of the common faith of the two churches.[20]

Another significant christological text was issued in June 1984, at
the conclusion of the visit of Syrian Orthodox Patriarch Ignatius
Zakka I Iwas to Rome. The Pope and Patriarch maintained in their
*Common Declaration* that past schisms "in no way affect or touch the
substance of their faith," since the divisions arose from terminologi-
cal misunderstandings. They then made a joint confession of faith in
the mystery of the Word made flesh in these words:

---

[18] "Communiqué," *Wort und Wahrheit* Supplementary Issue No. 2 (Vienna:
Herder, 1974) 175-176.

[19] Ibid., 176.

[20] *Information Service* 52 (1983/III) 74.

In our turn we confess that He became incarnate for us, taking to himself a real body with a rational soul. He shared our humanity in all things but sin. We confess that our Lord and our God, our Saviour and the King of all, Jesus Christ, is perfect God as to His divinity and perfect man as to His humanity. This Union is real, perfect, without blending or mingling, without confusion, without alteration, without division, without the least separation. He who is God eternal and invisible, became visible in the flesh and took the form of servant. In him are united, in a real, perfect indivisible and inseparable way, divinity and humanity, and in him all their properties are present and active.[21]

The christological agreement with the Coptic Orthodox Church was reaffirmed by Catholic and Coptic representatives meeting at Amba Bishoy Monastery in February 1988. They also adopted this more concise formulation which was intended to make the christological accord more accessible to the faithful:

We believe that our Lord, God and Saviour Jesus Christ, the Incarnate-Logos, is perfect in His Divinity and perfect in His Humanity. He made His Humanity One with His Divinity without Mixture, nor Mingling, nor Confusion. His Divinity was not separated from His Humanity even for a moment or twinkling of an eye. At the same time, we Anathematize the Doctrines of both Nestorius and Eutyches.[22]

This progress on christology was noted with satisfaction by the participants at the Fifth *Pro Oriente* Consultation in September 1988. They went on to emphasize

that the great mystery of the Incarnation of the Son of God could not be exhaustively formulated in words, and that within the limits of condemned errors like Arianism, Nestorianism and Eutycheanism, a certain plurality of expressions was permissible in relation to the inseparable and unconfused hypostatic unity of the human and the divine in one Lord Jesus Christ, the Word of God incarnate by the Holy Spirit of the Blessed Virgin Mary, con-

---

[21] *Information Service* 55 (1984/II-III) 62.

[22] *Information Service* 69 (1989/1) 8.

substantial with God the Father in His divinity and consubstantial with us in his humanity.[23]

Another christological agreement was reached at the first meeting of the new Joint International Commission for Dialogue between the Roman Catholic Church and the Malankara Syrian Orthodox Church of India, which was held at Kottayam in October 1989.[24] The statement, which was officially approved by the authorities of both churches and published on 3 June 1990, includes this text on the relationship between Christ's humanity and divinity in paragraph 5:

> Our Lord Jesus Christ is one, perfect in his humanity and perfect in his divinity, at once consubstantial with the Father in his divinity, and consubstantial with us in his humanity. His humanity is one with his divinity — without change, without commingling, without division and without separation. In the Person of the Eternal Logos Incarnate are united and active in a real and perfect way the divine and human natures, with all their properties, facul-. ties and operations.[25]

This put an end to any christological disagreement between the Catholic and Malankara Orthodox Syrian Churches.

A careful reading of these statements issued over the past twenty-five years indicates that the ancient christological dispute between the Oriental Orthodox Churches and the Catholic Church has been substantially resolved. Even though different interpretations of the meaning of the Chalcedonian definition remain, the churches have been able to set aside the old disputes and affirm that their faith in the mystery of Christ which transcends all formulations is, in fact, the same.

---

[23] "Communiqué," *Wort und Wahrheit*, Supplementary Issue No. 5 (Vienna: Herder, 1989) 149.

[24] See G. Daucourt, "First meeting for dialogue with Syrian Orthodox Church of India," *L'Osservatore Romano*, English weekly edition, 27 November 1989, p. 2.

[25] *L'Osservatore Romano* 3 June 1990, 5.

## Ecclesiology

Progress has also been made in the area of ecclesiology, although certain differences remain to be resolved. The nature of an ecumenical council has figured prominently in the theological discussion, since the Oriental Orthodox have received only the first three of the seven ancient councils accepted by the Catholic and Orthodox Churches. The concept and exercise of primacy is another area of disagreement, especially since the Oriental Orthodox have no experience of primacy among their five independent churches. Not even a limited form of primacy exists similar to the role that the Patriarchate of Constantinople plays among the Orthodox Churches. A third sensitive area is the existence of the Eastern Catholic Churches and the related question of proselytism between members of the two communions.

But before examining these areas of disparity, it is necessary to review the way in which both churches have consistently stated their recognition of the ecclesial reality of the other. Statements of this type are found at the very beginning of the series of visits between Popes and Oriental Orthodox hierarchs. In May 1970, when Catholicos Vasken I visited Pope Paul VI, he said, "We have remembered, as in a reawakening, that we have been brothers for the past two thousand years."[26] Paul VI responded:

> Let us give thanks to the Lord together that day by day the profound sacramental reality existing between our churches is made known to us, beyond the daily differences and the hostilities of the past.[27]

And in their *Common Declaration* at the conclusion of the visit, the two church leaders affirmed that collaboration and research

---

[26] *Information Service* 11 (1970/III) 9.
[27] Ibid.

must be founded on reciprocal recognition of the Christian faith and of common sacramental life, on mutual respect of persons and of their Churches.[28]

The *Common Declaration* of Paul VI and Coptic Pope Shenouda III in May 1973 stated that Catholics and Copts are re-discovering each other as churches despite the divisions of the past:

> These differences cannot be ignored. In spite of them, however, we are rediscovering ourselves as churches with a common inheritance and are reaching out with determination and confidence in the Lord to achieve the fullness and perfection of that unity which is His gift.[29]

During his visit to Istanbul in 1979, John Paul II spoke to Armenian Patriarch Shnork of "the unity which already exists between us." And in response, Patriarch Shnork indicated that both are parts of the one Church:

> Such visits serve the praiseworthy purpose of deepening the love, respect, and mutual understanding between various parts of the Christian Church. We shall always pray that God may bless this renewal of relations, which is manifested through such visits.[30]

This recognition of the full ecclesial reality of both churches has been stated repeatedly during subsequent visits and in common declarations. For instance, John Paul II said to Ethiopian Orthodox Patriarch Tekle Haimanot in 1981 that

> The contacts which we have reestablished are now enabling us to rediscover the profound and true reality of this existing unity. Even the real divergences between us are being seen more clearly as we gradually free them from so many secondary elements that derive from ambiguities of language.[31]

---

[28] *Acta Apostolicae Sedis* 62 (1970) 416.

[29] *Acta Apostolicae Sedis* 65 (1973) 300-301.

[30] *Information Service* 41 (1979/IV) 28.

[31] *Information Service* 47 (1981/III-IV) 100.

In later pronouncements, John Paul II and heads of Oriental Orthodox churches have listed areas of cooperation which this rediscovered relationship makes possible. In the *Joint Communiqué* issued at the end of the visit of Armenian Catholicos Karekine II of Cilicia to Rome in April 1983, cooperation was encouraged in the theological formation of clerics and laity, catechetical instruction, practical solutions of situations of common pastoral concern, social action, cultural promotion, and humanitarian services.[32]

In the *Common Declaration* of Pope John Paul II and Patriarch Ignatius Zakka I Iwas of June 1984, the two churches were considered so close that even cooperation in pastoral care was envisaged, including some sacramental sharing:

> It is not rare, in fact, for our faithful to find access to a priest of their own Church materially or morally impossible. Anxious to meet their needs and with their spiritual benefit in mind, we authorize them in such cases to ask for the sacraments of Penance, Eucharist, and Anointing of the Sick from lawful priests of either of our two sister Churches, when they need them.[33]

The historic nature of this declaration goes without saying. It is the first time in modern history that the Catholic Church and a church separated from it have agreed together to allow some forms of sacramental sharing.

In addition, the same declaration envisages cooperation in the formation and education of clergy:

> It would be a logical corollary of collaboration in pastoral care to cooperate in priestly formation and theological education. Bishops are encouraged to promote sharing of facilities for theological education where they judge it to be advisable.[34]

All this was made possible because of the Pope and Patriarch's common wish

---

[32] *Information Service* 51 (1983/I-II) 40.

[33] *Information Service* 55 (1984/II-III) 63.

[34] Ibid.

to widen the horizon of their brotherhood and affirm herewith the terms of the deep spiritual communion which already unites them and the prelates, clergy, and faithful of both their churches, to consolidate these ties of Faith, Hope, and Love, and to advance in finding a wholly common ecclesial life.[35]

It has become commonplace in recent speeches and common declarations to state that what unites the churches is far greater than that which divides, and to list common elements such as belief in the Trinity, the mystery of Christ, the apostolic traditions, the sacraments, the Theotokos, and especially the first three Ecumenical Councils.

In spite of all this, important areas of disagreement remain. Ecclesiological questions were considered for the first time at the second *Pro Oriente* theological consultation in 1973, and the third and fourth meetings were devoted entirely to this area. Ecclesiological issues also figured prominently at the fifth meeting.

The communiqué of the second consultation treated the question of ecumenical councils and the relationship between the papacy and councils in a tentative way. The members agreed that the first three councils have a "greater degree of fullness" because of their wider acceptance by Christians. Moreover, they "look forward to future regional and ecumenical councils with larger representation as the reunion of churches is hastened by the working of the Holy Spirit." On the relationship between Pope and Council, they praised the notion of collegiality expressed in the documents of Vatican II as "a move in the right direction according to which the role of the bishop of Rome is seen within the Council and not above it."[36]

The theologians were able to reach greater consensus on these issues in 1976 at the third *Pro Oriente* meeting. The communiqué described areas of agreement on the nature of the Church and the notion of conciliarity. The text begins by affirming that unity is Christ's gift to the Church. This is a unity which allows for a

---

[35] Ibid., 62.

[36] "Communiqué," *Wort und Wahrheit* Supplementary Issue No. 2 (Vienna: Herder, 1974) 176.

"multiplicity of traditions," where "diversity has to be held together by basic unity in fundamental matters."

The communiqué goes on to speak of the identity of the local and universal churches:

> One and same Church, for there cannot be more than one, is manifested both locally and universally as a koinonia of truth and love, characterized by eucharistic communion and the corporate unity of the episcopate. The unity of the Church has its source and prototype in the unity of the Father, the Son and the Holy Spirit, into which we have been baptized.[37]

Conciliarity is described as

> the understanding of the Church as koinonia, so essential to the nature of the Church as the Body of Christ, and so clearly visible in the structure of its life and leadership from the very inception.[38]

The communiqué considers the council or synod both as a single event and as a continuing structure of the Church's life. Insofar as it is an event, the theologians

> could not agree on how and by whom such a world-wide council of our churches should be convoked and conducted, nor could we agree completely on the procedure for the reception of past or future councils.[39]

Nevertheless, they agreed that churches have the right to convoke a council

> whenever found necessary and possible though there is no necessity to hold ecumenical councils at given intervals as a permanent structure of the Church. We recognize the need of structures of coordination between the autocephalous churches for the settle-

---

[37] "Communiqué," *Wort und Wahrheit* Supplementary Issue No. 3 (Vienna: Herder, 1976) 223.

[38] Ibid.

[39] Ibid.

ment of disputes and for facing together the problems and tasks confronting our churches in the modern world.[40]

The question of councils was taken up again in the communiqué issued by the fifth consultation in 1988. It reaffirms that the first three ecumenical councils provided the basis for the common faith of Catholics and Oriental Orthodox, and acknowledged that the Oriental Orthodox are "not in a position formally to accept" the Council of Chalcedon and the ones following it. However, further study of the later councils was recommended. The nature of the reception of conciliar teaching was also examined, and recognized to be a complex process which sometimes does not include formal reception of conciliar decisions as such.[41]

The fourth consultation (September 1978) discussed two more problems which divide the Catholic and Oriental Orthodox Churches: the notion of primacy and the status of Eastern Catholic Churches. Primacy was taken up again at the fifth meeting.

The communiqué of the fourth consultation describes primacy in the context of what it calls three integrally related elements in the life of the Church: primacy, conciliarity, and the consensus of the believing community. It recognizes, however, that "their relative importance has been differently understood in different situations."

The Oriental Orthodox understand primacy as being "of historical and ecclesiological origin," while Catholics see it as part of "the divine plan for the Church." Yet both sides acknowledge that primacy is connected with the continuing guidance of the Holy Spirit within the Church. The Catholic teachings about the primacy of the bishop of Rome

> are to be understood in the context of their historical, sociological and political conditions and also in the light of the historical

---

[40] Ibid., 223-224.

[41] "Communiqué," *Wort und Wahrheit*, Supplementary Issue Number 5 (Vienna: Herder, 1989) 149-50.

evolution of the whole teaching of the Roman Church, a process which is still continuing.[42]

The Oriental Orthodox, on the other hand,

> have not felt it necessary to formulate verbally and declare their understanding of primacy though it is clearly implied in the continuing life and teaching of their churches.[43]

The consultation called for more research and reflection on primacy "with a new vision for our future unity."

With regard to infallibility, both sides affirmed that it "pertains to the Church as a whole." But they could not agree on "the relative importance of different organs in the Church through which this inerrant teaching authority is to find expression."

The participants stated that Catholics and Oriental Orthodox should strive towards a goal of

> full union of sister churches — with communion in the faith, in the sacraments of the Church, in ministry and within a canonical structure. Each Church as well as all churches together will have a primatial and conciliar structure, providing for their communion in a given place as well as on regional and world-wide scale.[44]

The statements goes on to address the issue of a focus of such communion, and the role that Rome might play in it:

> The structure will be basically conciliar. No single Church in this communion will by itself be regarded as the source and origin of that communion; the source of the unity of the Church is the action of the triune God, Father, Son and Holy Spirit. It is the same Spirit who operates in all sister churches the same faith, hope and love, as well as ministry and sacraments. About regarding one particular Church as the center of the unity, there was no agree-

---

[42] "Communiqué," *Wort und Wahrheit*, Supplementary Issue Number 4 (Vienna: Herder, 1978) 233.

[43] Ibid.

[44] Ibid.

ment, though the need of a special ministry for unity was recognized by all.

This communion will find diverse means of expression — the exchange of letters of peace among the churches, the public liturgical remembering of the churches and their primates by each other, the placing of responsibility for convoking general synods in order to deal with common concerns of the churches, and so on.[45]

At the fifth consultation in 1988 the members recognized that both the Catholic and Oriental Orthodox churches possess some form of primacy, always related to the conciliar nature of the Church. While in the Catholic Church the Bishop of Rome's primacy serves the unity of all the churches, the Oriental Orthodox experience primacy only within each of their five independent churches, not at a level above them. Further study of this question was recommended. They acknowledged that in practice some form of both central coordination and local autonomy were needed.[46]

This lack of full agreement on the function of conciliarity and primacy within the Church explains why these topics are almost never mentioned in the speeches and common declarations that issued from visits between Popes and heads of Oriental Orthodox churches. The 1973 *Common Declaration* of Pope Paul VI and Pope Shenouda III contains the broad sentence, "We have, to a large degree, the same understanding of the Church, founded upon the Apostles, and of the important role of ecumenical and local councils."[47] The fact that nothing more specific could be said indicates the continuing divergence in the two churches' understanding of this important area in ecclesial life. In fact, after the 1973 meeting between Paul VI and Shenouda III, there were no visits between a Pope and the head of an Oriental Orthodox church for six years. The next contact took the form of the visit of a Coptic Orthodox delegation to John Paul II in 1979. The delegation carried a letter from Shenouda to

---

[45] Ibid.

[46] "Communiqué," *Wort und Wahrheit*, Supplementary Issue Number 5, (Vienna: Herder, 1989) 150.

[47] *Acta Apostolicae Sedis* 65 (1973) 300.

John Paul in which he expressed his concern about the lack of progress in the area of ecclesiology.

The 1973 *Common Declaration* had set up a special Joint Commission between the Catholic and Coptic Orthodox Churches to

> guide common study in the fields of Church tradition, patristics, liturgy, theology, history and practical problems, so that by cooperation in common we may seek to resolve, in a spirit of mutual respect, the differences existing between our churches.[48]

By 1979, this Commission had met four times in Cairo,[49] and had continued to make progress in the area of christology. But, as Pope Shenouda wrote in his letter to John Paul,

> In ecclesiology only very little real progress has been reached. This is why we thought it appropriate to delegate an official delegation of six members of the official Commission, in order to enhance the negotiations between our two churches, which seem to have stopped at a point without reaching further steps of real progress in the achievement of the unity of our two churches.[50]

In his speech to the delegation, Pope John Paul replied to some of the concerns raised in Pope Shenouda's letter. Although he did not address the question of conciliarity, he did speak briefly about the role of the papacy in the dialogue:

> I know that one of the fundamental questions of the ecumenical movement is the nature of that full communion we are seeking with each other and the role that the Bishop of Rome has to play, by God's design, in serving that communion of faith and spiritual

---

[48] Ibid., 301.

[49] On these meetings, see the following reports in *Proche Orient Chrétien*: "La commission mixte de l'Église copte orthodoxe et de l'Église catholique," 24 (1974) 68-69; "Première réunion de la commission mixte des Églises catholique et copte orthodoxe," 24 (1974) 175-178; "Deuxième réunion de la commission mixte," 25 (1975) 314-316; "[Troisième] Réunion de la commission mixte," 26 (1976) 360-361; "[Quatrième] Réunion de la commission mixte," 29 (1979) 107-109.

[50] *Information Service* 41 (1979/IV) 8.

life, which is nourished by the sacraments and expressed in fraternal charity. A great deal of progress has been made in deepening our understanding of this question. Much remains to be done. I consider your visit to me and to the See of Rome a significant contribution towards resolving this question definitively.[51]

One could raise a question about how Pope John Paul understood the visit of the Coptic delegation to Rome as "a significant contribution towards resolving this question definitively." Perhaps this is an example of the kind of communion he would envisage taking place after the reestablishment of unity: occasional official visits between heads of sister churches to inform the universal primate about the life of their churches, something along the lines of the means of expression of communion outlined in the fourth *Pro Oriente* communiqué.

In the same speech, Pope John Paul emphasized that the reestablishment of communion between the churches would not imply the loss of the identity of either of them:

> Fundamental to this dialogue is the recognition that the richness of this unity in faith and spiritual life has to be expressed in diversity of forms. Unity — whether on the universal level or the local level — does not mean uniformity or absorption of one group by another. It is rather at the service of all groups to help each live better the proper gifts it has received from God's Spirit. . . . With no one trying to dominate each other but to serve each other, all together will grow into that perfection of unity for which Our Lord prayed on the night before he died.[52]

Unfortunately, the political situation in Egypt worsened soon after this visit, and Pope Shenouda was placed under house arrest by President Sadat in September 1981. This brought the dialogue between the Catholic and Coptic Orthodox Churches to a virtual

---

[51] Ibid., 7.
[52] Ibid.

standstill. It was only after Pope Shenouda's release in January 1985 that the commission could resume its work.[53]

In their *Common Declaration* of June 1984, Pope John Paul II and Syrian Patriarch Ignatius Zakka I Iwas added some significant new elements to the developing ecclesiological consensus between the two churches. The declaration seems to have drawn from the work of other interconfessional dialogues, and places the Eucharist at the center of its understanding of the Church. Here the Eucharist is shown to be much more than one of the seven sacraments that Catholics and Syrian Orthodox have in common:

> Sacramental life finds in the Holy Eucharist its fulfillment and its summit, in such a way that it is through the Eucharist that the Church most profoundly realizes and reveals its nature. . . . The other Sacraments . . . are ordered to that celebration of the holy Eucharist which is the centre of sacramental life and the chief visible expression of ecclesial communion. This communion of Christians with each other and of local churches united around their lawful Bishops is realized in the gathered community which confesses the same faith.[54]

---

[53] The first phase of the commission's work was concluded with the adoption of a brief christological statement in 1988. The second phase, which was to examine other issues, began with the commission's fifth meeting at Amba Bishoy monastery in October 1988. The discussion at this meeting centered on the mystery of the redemption and the final destiny of the human person. See report in *Irénikon* 61 (1988) 537-539, *Information Service* 68 (1988/III-IV) 164, and *Proche Orient Chrétien* 39 (1989) 330-333. The sixth session, which took place at the same monastery in April 1990, discussed the procession of the Holy Spirit and the *filioque*. See *Proche Orient Chrétien* 40 (1990) 301-303, and *Irénikon* 63 (1990) 213-215. The seventh session, held in April 1991, studied the situation of the faithful after death and the Catholic teaching on Purgatory. It also set up a joint pastoral commission to deal with concrete local problems involving the faithful of the two communities. See *Irénikon* 64 (1991) 236-237, and *Proche Orient Chrétien* 41 (1991) 362-364. The discussion continued at the eighth meeting in February 1992: *Irénikon* 65 (1992) 63-65. The ninth meeting, scheduled for April 1993, had to be cancelled because of technical difficulties.

[54] *Information Service* 55 (1984/II-III) 62.

This is the first time that a common declaration makes such a connection between Church, Eucharist, and Bishop. It represents an ecclesiological advance which needs to be amplified in future statements.

Another question which has arisen in relations between Catholics and Oriental Orthodox concerns the Eastern Catholic Churches. Until recently, the Catholic Church has presented these churches as a model of the relationship which should exist between itself and any eastern church which might come into communion with it.[55] The Oriental Orthodox, on the other hand, tend to take great offense at the very existence of these churches, because they are often the direct result of Catholic missionary activity among the Oriental Orthodox faithful. They see in this a denial of the ecclesial reality of the Oriental Orthodox Churches by the Catholic Church, and claim that some Eastern Catholics continue to proselytize even now among the Oriental Orthodox faithful.

The first mention of the Eastern Catholic Churches in the encounters between Popes and Oriental Orthodox hierarchs is found in the speech Paul VI delivered in the presence of Armenian Catholicos of Cilicia Khoren I in May 1967. Perhaps not attuned to Oriental Orthodox sensitivities in this matter, the Pope expressed his affection for the Armenian tradition by recalling the *Decree for the Armenians* of the Council of Florence, the foundation of the Armenian College in Rome, the Armenian Catholic presence in Venice, and highly-placed Armenian Catholics in the Roman Curia.[56] He did the same in a speech during the visit of Catholicos Vasken I of Etchmiadzin in 1970.[57]

---

[55] See letter of Cardinal Willebrands to Russian Orthodox Metropolitan Juvenaly of September 22, 1979, where, in the context of a misunderstanding about a papal statement on the status of the Ukrainian Catholic Church, the Cardinal wrote, "There was no intention whatever of presenting the Union of Brest as the model for our relations with the Orthodox Churches today or as one for the contemplated future union." Text in T. Stransky and J. Sheerin, *Doing the Truth in Charity* (Ramsey: Paulist, 1982) 228.

[56] *Acta Apostolicae Sedis* 59 (1967) 511-512.

[57] *Information Service* 11 (1970/III) 5.

This problem was mentioned in an indirect way in the *Common Declaration* of Paul VI and Shenouda III in 1973 when they rejected all forms of proselytism as incompatible with the relationship that should exist between the two churches:

> . . . We reject all forms of proselytism, in the sense of acts by which persons seek to disturb each other's communities by recruiting new members from each other through methods, or because of attitudes of mind, which are opposed to the exigencies of Christian love or to what should characterize the relationships between churches. Let it cease, where it may exist.[58]

This statement was a response to Pope Shenouda's complaint that Coptic Catholics were proselytizing among Coptic Orthodox in Egypt. The Coptic Catholic Patriarch was reminded of this statement in a letter from Pope Paul soon thereafter.[59]

This issue has not been taken up in any of the speeches and common declarations since 1973. However, the fourth *Pro Oriente* meeting of 1978 made this statement about the status of these churches:

> The Oriental Catholic Churches will not even in the transitional period before full unity be regarded as a device for bringing Oriental Orthodox Churches inside the Roman Communion. Their role will be more in terms of collaborating in the restoration of eucharistic communion among the sister churches. The Oriental Orthodox Churches, according to the principles of Vatican II and subsequent statements of the See of Rome cannot be fields of mission for other churches. The sister churches will work out local solutions, in accordance with differing local situations, implementing as far as possible the principle of a unified episcopate for each locality.[60]

---

58 *Acta Apostolicae Sedis* 65 (1973) 301.

59 "Lettre du Pape Paul VI au Patriarche copte catholique," *Proche Orient Chrétien* 24 (1974) 351-354.

60 "Communiqué," *Wort und Wahrheit* Supplementary Issue No. 4 (Vienna: Herder, 1978) 233-234.

The position of the Catholic Church which emerges from these statements is twofold. While it affirms the right of the Eastern Catholic Churches to exist, it also gives assurances that Catholics are not to proselytize among Oriental Orthodox Christians. Even so, many Oriental Orthodox remain suspicious of the true intentions of their Eastern Catholic counterparts, and continue to feel that these churches are made up of their own faithful which have been unjustly taken away from them.

The contemporary relationship between the Catholic and Oriental Orthodox Churches is unique, and the resolution of the christological divergences between the two communions is unprecedented. In no other ecumenical relationship has a dogmatic disagreement of this type been overcome so unequivocally, and with such official approbation. This was achieved without any official bilateral dialogue taking place.[61] The interplay of unofficial theological consultations and official pronouncements made by Church leaders proved to be an effective means of resolving a centuries-old problem.

At the same time, the lack of any clearly defined ministry serving the unity of the various Oriental Orthodox Churches has necessitated a rather piecemeal process by which levels of agreement with individual churches differ. The lack of a specific christological accord with the Armenian or Ethiopian churches somewhat relativizes the importance of the accord reached with the Copts, Syrians and Malankaras. Nevertheless, progress has been substantial and provides real hope for the future.

Ecclesiology remains the area which contains the greatest disagreement. It is doubtful that any of the Oriental Orthodox Churches will accept any form of unity with the Catholic Church which does not fully respect their administrative independence. And the Catholic Church must decide if full communion with another

---

[61] It should be noted that the fifth *Pro Oriente* consultation in 1988 "urgently appeals to all the churches represented here to set up a joint official body to engage in that formal dialogue between the Roman Catholic Church and the family of the Oriental Orthodox Churches which will have as its objective the achieving of full communion in faith and sacramental life." See text in *Wort und Wahrheit*, Supplementary Issue No. 5, (Vienna: Herder, 1989) 151.

Church necessarily means that the Bishop of Rome must have unlimited authority to intervene in the affairs of the other church. These issues will provide ample material for research and reflection in the years to come as the relationship between these churches reaches greater maturity.

## Official Visits: Popes and Oriental Orthodox Hierarchs

1. Armenian Catholicos Khoren I to Paul VI
   Rome, May 9, 1967
   2 Speeches
   *Acta Apostolicae Sedis* 59 (1967) 510-12
   *L'Osservatore Romano* (May 10, 1967) 1

2. Paul VI to Patriarch Shnork Kalustian
   Istanbul, July 25-26, 1967
   2 Speeches
   *Information Service* (1967/3) 13-14

3. Armenian Catholicos Vasken I to Paul VI
   Rome, May 8-12, 1970
   a) 4 Speeches
   *Information Service* 11 (1970/III) 3-10
   b) Common Declaration
   *Acta Apostolicae Sedis* 62 (1970) 416-7

(First *Pro Oriente* Theological Consultation:
   Vienna, Austria September 7-12, 1971)

4. Syrian Patriarch Ignatius Yacoub III to Paul VI
   Rome, October 25-27, 1971
   a) 4 Speeches
   *Information Service* 16 (1972/I) 3-5
   b) Common Declaration
   *Acta Apostolicae Sedis* 63 (1971) 814-815

5. Coptic Pope Shenouda III to Paul VI
   Rome, May 4-10, 1973
   a) 8 Speeches
      *Information Service* 22 (1973/IV) 3-10
   b) Common Declaration
      *Acta Apostolicae Sedis* 65 (1973) 299-301

(Second *Pro Oriente* Theological Consultation:
   Vienna, Austria, September 3-9, 1973)

(Third *Pro Oriente* Theological Consultation:
   Vienna, Austria, August 30 to September 5, 1976)

(Fourth *Pro Oriente* Theological Consultation:
   Vienna, Austria, September 11-17, 1978)

6. Reception of Coptic Delegation by John Paul II
   Rome, June 23, 1979
   a) Letter from Pope Shenouda
   b) Speech by John Paul II
      *Information Service* 41 (1979/IV) 6-8

7. John Paul II to Armenian Patriarch Shnork
   Istanbul, November 29, 1979
   2 Speeches
      *Information Service* 41 (1979/IV) 28-29

8. Syrian Patriarch Ignatius Yacoub III to John Paul II
   Rome, May 13-16, 1980
   4 Speeches
      *Information Service* 44 (1980/III-IV) 92-95

9. Reception of Ethiopian Orthodox Delegation by John Paul II
   Rome, July 16-19, 1980
   Two Letters
      *Information Service* 44 (1980/III-IV) 97-98

10. Ethiopian Patriarch Tekle Haimanot to John Paul II
    Rome, October 17, 1981
    2 Speeches
    *Information Service* 47 (1981/III-IV) 100-101

11. Armenian Catholicos Karekine II to John Paul II
    Rome, April 15-19, 1983
    a) 2 Speeches
    b) Joint Communiqué
       *Information Service* 51 (1983/I-II) 37-41

12. Syrian Catholicos of India Moran Mar Baselius Marthoma
    Mathews I to John Paul II
    Rome, June 2-5, 1983
    2 Speeches
    *Information Service* 52 (1983/III) 72-75

13. Syrian Patriarch Ignatius Zakka I Iwas to John Paul II
    Rome, June 20-23, 1984
    a) 2 Speeches
    b) Common Declaration
       *Information Service* 55 (1984/II-III) 59-63

14. Pope John Paul II to Mar Basileus Paulos II, Catholicos of the
    Malankara Jacobite Syrian Orthodox Church
    Kottayam, India, February 7, 1986
    Speech of Pope John Paul II
       *Information Service* 60 (1986/I-II) 12-13

15. Pope John Paul II to Syrian Catholicos of India Moran Mar
    Baselius Marthoma Mathews I
    Kottayam, India, February 8, 1986
    a) Speech of Pope John Paul II
       *Information Service* 60 (1986/I-II) 13-14
       *Star of the East* 8 (1986) 8-9
    b) Speech of Catholicos Marthoma Matthews I

*The Star of the East* 8 (1986) 5-7

(Fifth "Pro Oriente" Theological Consultation:
   Vienna, Austria September 18-25, 1988)

16. Ethiopian Patriarch Abuna Paulos to John Paul II
      Rome, June 11, 1993
      Speech of Pope John Paul II
         *L'Osservatore Romano*, 11-12 June 1993, p. 4

# BIBLIOGRAPHY

This bibliography contains only the major works that were consulted in compiling this book, plus a limited selection of books in English on various aspects of the Eastern Churches for further reading.

*Anglican-Orthodox Dialogue: The Dublin Agreed Statement 1984.* London: SPCK, 1985. Contains all Anglican-Orthodox agreed statements from 1976 onwards.

*Annuario Pontificio 1993.* Vatican City: Editrice Vaticana, 1993.

Atiya, A. *A History of Eastern Christianity.* London: Methuen & Co., 1968. A history of the Assyrian and Oriental Orthodox Churches.

Attwater, Donald. *The Christian Churches of the East* (2 Volumes). Milwaukee: Bruce, 1961.

*Autocephaly: The Orthodox Church in America.* Crestwood, New York: St. Vladimir's, 1971. Documentation and essays on the status of the OCA from an OCA perspective.

Barrett, D., ed. *World Christian Encyclopedia.* Oxford: Oxford University Press, 1982. Exhaustive statistical presentation of Christianity in every country.

Betts, R.B. *Christians in the Arab East.* Athens: Lycabettus, 1978.

Bolshakoff, S. *Russian Mystics.* Kalamazoo: Cistercian Publications, 1980.

Bria, I., ed. *Martyria/Mission: The Witness of the Orthodox Churches Today.* Geneva: WCC, 1980.

Bulgakov, S. *The Orthodox Church.* Revised translation by L. Kesich. Crestwood, NY: St. Vladimir's, 1988.

Cabasilas, Nicholas. *The Life in Christ*. Crestwood, NY: St. Vladimir's, 1974. Classic 14th century work on liturgical/sacramental spirituality.

Chrysostomos, Bishop, with Bishop Auxentios and Archimandrite Ambrosios, *The Old Calendar Orthodox Church of Greece*. Etna, California: Center for Tradtionalist Orthodox Studies, 1991.

*Code of Canons of the Eastern Churches: Latin-English Edition*. Washington, DC: Canon Law Society of America, 1992.

Constantelos, D. *Understanding the Greek Orthodox Church: Its Faith, History and Practice*. New York: Seabury, 1982.

Cragg, Kenneth, *The Arab Christian: A History in the Middle East*. London: Mowbray, 1991.

Daniel, David. *The Orthodox Church of India*. New Delhi: Miss Rachel David, 1972.

Δίπτυχα τῆς Ἐκκλησίας τῆς Ἑλλάδος 1993. Athens: Apostoliki Diakonia, 1992.

*Directory of Orthodox Parishes and Clergy in the British Isles 1988/89*. Welshpool: Stylite Publishing, 1988.

Dvornik, F. *Byzantium and the Roman Primacy*. New York: Fordham University Press, 1966.

Efthimiou, M., and G. Christopoulos. *A History of the Greek Orthodox Church in America*. New York: Greek Orthodox Archdiocese, 1984.

Ellis, J. *The Russian Orthodox Church: A Contemporary History*. London and Sydney: Croom Helm, 1986.

Every, G. *Understanding Eastern Christianity*. Bangalore: Dharmaram Publications, 1978.

Fortescue, A. *The Lesser Eastern Churches*. London: Catholic Truth Society, 1913.

Fries, Paul and Tiran Nersoyan, eds. *Christ in East and West*. Macon, Georgia: Mercer University Press, 1987.

Geanakoplos, Deno, *A Short History of the Ecumenical Patriarchate of Constantinople (330-1990): "First Among Equals" in the Eastern Orthodox Church*. Brookline, Massachusetts: Holy Cross Orthodox Press, 1990.

Gill, J. *The Council of Florence*. Cambridge: Cambridge University Press, 1959.

Gregorios, P., W. Lazareth, N. Nissiotis, eds. *Does Chalcedon Divide or Unite? Towards Convergence in Orthodox Christology*. Geneva: World Council of Churches, 1981. Essays on the christological and ecclesiological issues that divide the Orthodox Church from the Oriental Orthodox Churches.

Hill, H., ed. *Light from the East: A Symposium on the Oriental Orthodox and Assyrian Churches*. Toronto: Anglican Book Centre, 1988.

Horner, N. *A Guide to Christian Churches in the Middle East*. Elkhart, IN: Mission Focus, 1989.

Hussey, J. M. *The Orthodox Church in the Byzantine Empire*. Oxford: Claredon Press, 1986.

Janin, R. *Églises orientales et rites orientaux*. Paris: Letouzey & Ané, 1955.

Kilmartin, E. *Toward Reunion: The Orthodox and Roman Catholic Churches*. New York: Paulist Press, 1979.

Limouris, G., and N. Vaporis, eds. *Orthodox Perspectives on Baptism, Eucharist and Ministry*. Brookline, MA: Holy Cross, 1986.

Litsas, F., ed. *A Companion to the Greek Orthodox Church*. New York: Greek Orthodox Archdiocese, 1984.

Lossky, V. *The Mystical Theology of the Eastern Church*. Cambridge: James Clarke & Co., 1957.

Maloney, G. *A History of Orthodox Theology Since 1453*. Belmont, MA: Nordland, 1976.

Maximos, Metropolitan of Sardis. *The Oecumenical Patriarchate in the Orthodox Church: A Study in the History and Canons of the*

*Church.* Analekta Vlatadon 24. Thessalonika: Patriarchal Institute, 1976.

Meyendorff, J. *Byzantine Theology: Historical Trends and Doctrinal Themes.* New York: Fordham University Press, 1974.

Meyendorff, J. *The Orthodox Church.* Crestwood, NY: St. Vladimir's, 1981.

Meyendorff, J., et al. *The Primacy of Peter in the Orthodox Church.* Leighton Buzzard: The Faith Press, 1963.

Meyendorff, J. *A Study of Gregory Palamas.* Crestwood, NY: St. Vladimir's, 1974. Best study available in English on this crucial 14th century Byzantine theologian.

*Oriente cattolico: cenni storici e statistiche.* Vatican City: Congregation for Oriental Churches, 1974. Statistical and historical survey of all Eastern Catholic Churches.

*Orthodoxia 1992-1993.* Regensburg: Ostkirchliches Institut, 1992. A list with basic biographical information regarding all bishops of every non-Catholic eastern church.

Ouspensky, L., and V. Lossky. *The Meaning of Icons.* Revised edition, Crestwood, NY: St. Vladimir's, 1982.

Patelos, C., ed. *The Orthodox Church in the Ecumenical Movement: Documents and Statements 1902-1975.* Geneva: WCC, 1978.

Pelikan, J. *The Christian Tradition: A History of the Development of Doctrine.* Volume 2: *The Spirit of Eastern Christendom (600-1700).* Chicago: University of Chicago Press, 1974.

Pennington, B. *One Yet Two: Monastic Tradition East and West.* Kalamazoo, MI: Cistercian Publications, 1976. Papers from an Orthodox-Cistercian Symposium, 1973.

Podipara, P.J. *The Thomas Christians.* Bombay: St. Paul Publications, 1970.

Pospielovsky, D. *The Russian Church Under the Soviet Regime 1917-1982* (2 volumes). Crestwood, NY: St. Vladimir's, 1984.

Ramet, Pedro, ed. *Eastern Christianity and Politics in the Twentieth Century*. Durham and London: Duke University Press, 1988.

Runciman, S. *The Eastern Schism: A Study of the Papacy and the Eastern Churches During the XIth and XIIth Centuries*. Oxford: Clarendon Press, 1955.

Runciman, S. *The Great Church in Captivity: A Study of the Patriarchate of Constantinople from the Eve of the Turkish Conquest to the Greek War of Independence*. Cambridge: Cambridge University Press, 1968.

Schmemann, A. *For the Life of the World: Sacraments and Orthodoxy*. Crestwood, NY: St. Vladimir's, 1973.

Schmemann, A. *The Historical Road of Eastern Orthodoxy*. Crestwood, NY: St. Vladimir's, 1977.

Schulz, H. *The Byzantine Liturgy: Symbolic Structure and Faith Expression*. New York: Pueblo Publishing Company, 1986.

Špidlík, T. *The Spirituality of the Christian East: A Systematic Handbook*. Cistercian Studies 79. Kalamazoo, MI: Cistercian Publications, 1986.

Stormon, E., ed. *Towards the Healing of Schism: The Sees of Rome and Constantinople. Public Statements and Correspondence between the Holy See and the Ecumenical Patriarchate 1958-1984*. New York: Paulist, 1987.

Surrency, Archimandrite Serafim. *The Quest for Orthodox Unity in America. A History of the Orthodox Church in North America in the Twentieth Century*. New York: Sts. Boris and Gleb, 1973.

Taft, R. *The Liturgy of the Hours East and West: The Origins of the Divine Office and its Meaning for Today*. Collegeville, Minnesota: Liturgical Press, 1986.

Taft, R., ed. *The Oriental Orthodox Churches in the United States*. Washington: United States Catholic Conference, 1986.

van der Bent, A.J. *Handbook Member Churches: World Council of Churches*. Geneva: WCC, 1985.

Vischer, L. *Spirit of God, Spirit of Christ: Ecumenical Reflections on the Filioque Controversy*. London: SPCK, 1981.

Ware, Bishop Kallistos, ed. *The Art of Prayer: An Orthodox Anthology*. London: Faber and Faber, 1966.

Ware, Bishop Kallistos. *The Orthodox Church*. New York: Penguin Books, 1984 edition. A classic introduction to Orthodox history, theology, and worship.

Ware, Bishop Kallistos. *The Orthodox Way*. London: Mowbray & Co., 1979. The meaning of theology for spirituality.

*Yearbook 1992*. London: Greek Orthodox Archdiocese of Thyateira and Great Britain, 1991.

*Yearbook 1993*. New York: Greek Orthodox Archdiocese of North and South America, 1992.

Zizioulas, J. *Being as Communion: Studies in Personhood and the Church*. Crestwood, NY: St. Vladimir's, 1985.

# INDEX OF CHURCHES AND THEIR HEADS